COMA

Life in another time

Coma – *Life in another time*
by Arturo Croci

English paperback edition published by Patrician Press
in association with Arturo Croci 2019
Italian paperback edition by Patrician Press 2018
Copyright © 2018 Italian edition Arturo Croci
Copyright © 2019 English edition Arturo Croci

ISBN paperback Italian edition: 978-0-9955386-2 -7
ISBN paperback English edition: 978-1-9997030-7-3

www.patricianpress.com

COMA

Life in another time

Arturo Croci

Patrician Press
Manningtree

Published by Patrician Press
in association with Arturo Croci

Contents

Foreword

La morte si sconta vivendo (The price of life is death), is what one of the most important Italian poets, Giuseppe Ungaretti wrote in one of his most notable poems.

All that we, mere mortals, know for certain, is that at our end – sadly filled with a feeling of ineluctable defeat – the effect of death is in that cruel moment our being ceases.

But, in reality, only after we have crossed the landscape of life, will we participate, wrapped in darkness and silence, in the mysterious 'other side' – an other side that each one of us will reach in desperate and absolute loneliness.

Well, Arturo Croci (thanks to a ruthless adversary by the name of Aortic Aneurysm), imprisoned inside a hospital bed, was resigned, in spite of himself, to leave for that other side.

Perhaps, however, because he had not used up all the time allocated to him here – unexpectedly and temporarily – his departure was postponed.

With this additional time, he was able to give substance to his autobiographical novel, emblematically titled: *Coma – Life in another time.*

With *Coma*, Croci wanted to narrate his life by writing a story that otherwise would have vegetated in an inconsistent, endless dream, partly made of episodes relived and partly lived in another dimension. To achieve this, he used the technique of flash-back narrative, expertly combining episodes derived from reality and others immersed in 'fervent' fiction.

In this way, this flow of memories is transformed from being an evocation and explanation of an ordinary life, into a prodigiously extraordinary one.

The atmosphere one breathes from the pages of Coma is the powerful and overlying cry: *Viva la vita* with which Croci, waiting for the fateful afterlife, expresses for us mortals, a conscious will of revenge and of hope.

Angelo Lamberti

COMA
Life in another time

Introduction

The 105 mm cannonball goes directly to my heart; my chest and right arm hurt. I don't know exactly what's going on, however it's definitely something serious. I pick up the phone and call Gina, my wife, asking her to get help because I feel terrible. Italo, one of my colleagues, arrives and I tell him to leave: *This morning, no work!* he looks at me puzzled but then goes away, grumbling something I cannot understand.

I feel weaker and weaker, drops of cold sweat bead my forehead, I lie down on the ground; I feel my left leg disappearing, no longer responding to my commands.
Gina arrives and gets upset. Seeing me on the ground she puts a pillow under my head; the men in orange overalls from the emergency services arrive, they ask me what happened and how I feel. They transfer me to a stretcher. I take off my watch, I tell my wife that my health card is in my wallet, that the PIN of my phone is 22 33.
I lose consciousness; I am not aware of them taking me by ambulance from the office to the emergency room in the hospital in Merate.
I glimpse a doctor's face. He brings me back to consciousness just for a few minutes. I take off my rings by dribbling some saliva on my fingers – the doctor says he would cut them off otherwise as they were tight; however, they had been on my fingers for over 35 years. Elena, my niece, has tears in her eyes, and I ask her: *Why are you crying?* She replies with a sad voice *Because you are dying;* I smile, and I answer her: *You know, only 'hic et nunc' exists, here and now.*
I close my eyes and let myself go. From far, far away, I think I can hear the deafening noise of helicopter blades, but I don't really care.
Four weeks later they tell me what happened: an aneurysm with dissection of the aorta. The helicopter that should have taken me from the Emergency Room of Merate to the cardiology clinic of San

Donato Milanese, took me to Bergamo instead because of the fog. Now I know that the first person to save my life was a foreign doctor in the hospital in Merate: he understood I had problems with my aorta, he sedated and intubated me, applied a neuro-muscular block and prepared me for transport. If that doctor had made a mistake, I would not be here writing now. (Long afterwards I found out his name is Fritz Polo).

Gina is brought to the hospital (Ospedali Riuniti) together with my friend Franco Locatelli, who knows everything there is to know about Bergamo.

Prof. Aiazzi, head of vascular cardiology, shows my wife a box and says: *This is the prosthesis for your husband, it's just arrived from Milan, it costs over 20,000 euros. Madam there is no time left, please sign here.*

I am in a sort of orange thermal bag, at low temperature, already intubated, four surgeons and the team enter the operating room. It's 2.30 p.m, Gina sits on a bench and waits, it gets dark.

At about 8.00 p.m. Dr. Maurizio Tespili leaves the operating room and says: *Madam, I have done what I can, now we just have to wait and hope that everything goes well. If he survives the night, tomorrow we will return to the operating theatre for the leg bypass.*

Tespili makes a drawing of the aorta on a piece of paper, explaining that the aneurysm was at the bottom of the aortic arch, and that it is almost always fatal. Later I discover that none of the surgeons in the vascular cardiology department wanted the responsibility for operating and so in the end it was Dr. Maurizio Tespili – from the Hemodynamics Department – who tried.

Three weeks of pharmacological coma follow – as per the protocol of that period – the prosthesis placed in the aorta had to fit gradually, my blood pressure had to be kept low and there was frequent dialysis, however I have no consciousness of all these things. In the Intensive Care Unit, I was full of tubes, attached to machines that injected me with what was needed to keep me alive. Gina, with appropriate gowns and protection, could visit for five minutes a day. Once I saw her, but it was as if I was underwater, she was far away, evanescent and out of focus.

The cardiology clinic of Barcelona

All this was happening outside of me; inside I was living in a world of very strange reality. I was absolutely convinced that I had been admitted to the Cardiology Clinic in Barcelona and that an international group of doctors was taking care of me; it was led by Katrin Or, an Israeli doctor who was a fighter pilot. Katrin told me that her group was studying heart diseases and their origin, and that she had discovered that the HIV virus – or fragments of the modified virus – could cause various heart problems and that this fact was quite underestimated. She also told me that, in my case, the situation was evolving positively and that thanks to the therapies developed by her and her group I would soon be able to go home. The faces I remember are those of Gina and Elena – I wondered how they got to Barcelona. I also remember another female face, perhaps a nurse. There was also a boy who stood out, not very tall, with olive skin, in a white coat. The registered voice outside my mind is: *I'm Gina, do you recognise me?* Elena, on the other hand, was keeping her head down, and looked pensive and silent.

I remember the environment and the equipment they used. I was lying flat and machines were emitting flows that were sliding over me.
Barcelona is a city that has always fascinated me. The first time, at the University and, after that, many other times... how many?
I don't know exactly; I would say at least five, but... I had never heard of a Cardiology Clinic. When I was at the University, I visited the length and breadth of Barcelona, but I never knew if or where there was a Cardiology Clinic
I remember the entrance, the details of the flower beds, the main door and the corridors. I wondered: *How does Gina know I'm here? How did she find me in this hospital?* and then other questions, like *where is she going to eat and sleep in the evening?* Once I imagined following her, in the streets only faintly lit by street lamps, up to a building, not far from the hospital. It was a working class block of flats, with doors in glass and anodised aluminium, very common and maybe even a bit shabby... she had the key and went in. I calmed down and continued to sleep. At the hospital there was a special

section made up of young volunteers, some of them were going around the city to help people in need; they were often drunk, much more often having overdosed.

I can see two of them clearly and I listen to the dialogue in Catalan. What a strange language Catalan is; the first time at the University I was surprised. In part it resembles the dialect of Piacenza, the pronunciation is a bit different but many words, some close to French, others to Spanish, are similar. Actually, I can understand almost everything even if I find it hard to speak.

- *It can't go on like this, the number of drug addicts is increasing dramatically, and the use of certain synthetic substances is causing irreversible damage.*
- *We will never manage this, there aren't enough of us, resources are scarce... the authorities cannot expect the volunteers to solve this social scourge.*
- *We do what is possible and sometimes even what is impossible.*
- *Is there someone who really understands what we are doing?*
- *Will they sometimes say... thank you?*
- *I don't know, I do what I do because I think it's right to devote part of my time to others...*
- *And this makes you feel better... it satisfies your self-esteem...?*
- *Continuing to wonder why, why, why, is useless and leads us to the madhouse... two ambulances are coming... let's get this done.*

The reasons why people and especially young people use drugs are varied and complicated, however they clearly indicate that we are in a sick society. I tried to smoke weed once in Kandy, Sri-Lanka, but I ended up by throwing three quarters of the cigarette in the hotel's toilet, as it was causing me the devil of a headache, and since then I have not been tempted again. It also reminds me of what had happened to me and what I had written on my trip to New York.

New York reflections:
Thoughts on the search for freedom

The taxi that takes me from 37th Street in New York to the JFK airport leaves me with the typical scenario of big cities and a dead tramp on the sidewalk. Next to the body lying on cardboard there are a man and a woman; she cries. The bored policemen are waiting for the arrival of the coroner. I think, yes, one place is as good as another for dying, but I come from a different land and culture.

A little further on, at a traffic light, a guy on foot approaches the car window, saying he's got AIDS and asking for money; I dig into my pockets looking for a couple of dollars but I don't have time to take out the change, the taxi driver, angry at the red light, turns to me and says: *Just look around you, look carefully ... society here is not going well and it's not going anywhere.* The taxi driver is an Iranian student who, to pay for his studies, is working in his spare time.
I think that maybe he is right, however the Islamic model is not for me and therefore, to avoid unnecessary discussions, I keep quiet.
Here is Michael Jackson's apartment, there are already fans near the house who hope to see him, but he usually leaves with his helicopter from the roof. A little further are Broadway and Times Square, with shops full of all sorts of goods, and it does not matter if in New Jersey everything costs half the price, it's here where tourists from all over the world spend their money.

In Amsterdam, sometime later, I met Franco Bruno Gnisci, who received the Nobel Peace Prize in 1985 on behalf of the Association of Physicians against Nuclear War. He is living, taking advantage of what happened, without a fixed home. One day he is here, another elsewhere. He talks about peace and other things like that.
One evening, during a visit to Calco, he makes me look on the Internet for data on juvenile suicide. What I find leaves me, to say the least, shocked: every 17 minutes in the world, a young person, aged between 12 and 25, takes their own life.
The various statistics list the reasons for suicide for adults: alcohol, drug addiction, serious illness, loneliness. This is not true for young people and apparently no one is able to give an unequivocal

explanation. Going deeper into the various statistics it turns out that about 80-90% of youth suicides happen in the Western world; this means they are white and from wealthy families, so it is not the *poor* who take their own lives. Perhaps the poor still have something to conquer, something to achieve, but in any case, for them, life still seems to have a value.

I am in a bar in Vertemate, right in the middle of total chaos, thanks to the collapse of the Asian economy (I wonder how it happened so suddenly, without any media reporting it; in the months prior to the facts, there was no news that could have warned small investors: is it possible that nobody knew?).

In an ironic tone, a guy asked a poor fellow, who by eight in the morning had already drunk a couple of glasses of white wine, what he thought about the situation: *Let's see what you say about such an important fact, since you're always drunk and in vino veritas truth is found in wine.* The man's answer makes me think even today: *They have not yet understood that money cannot continue indefinitely to make more money, sooner or later someone has to DO the work.*

Like any citizen of this country, Europe and the world, I have seen several electoral campaigns, I have met kings, queens, actresses, ambassadors, spies, fixers, whores, homosexuals and important politicians, I have heard important and enlightened speeches.

I visited Moscow many years before the fall of the Berlin Wall.

I worked for many years in the European Association of Young Horticulturalists (*CEJH*), well before the European Union was born.

I saw the collapse of Communism and the birth of the global market.

Now, the most frequent word that appears in every speech, no matter which country you are in, is... Freedom.

Everyone knows the definition of freedom, even if by this term we mean something unlimited, which has no boundaries.

However, in reality, there are boundaries, and not just where the freedom of others begins. The most difficult borders to overcome are the mental ones.

The fundamental difference between Western philosophy, in other words, the one that originated in Greece with the government of the *Polis*, and the Eastern one, is simple: the western one has to do with closed places, delimitation of space (the city), while the eastern one addresses the whole.

In fact, with information technology and globalisation, Eastern philosophy was definitively defeated, as was Communism. From this, we can deduce, albeit summarily, that Western philosophy, in other words, our way of life, seems to be the winning model.

Is it winning?

This society, taking materialism to the limit, ignoring the values of life and of culture *is not heading in the right direction*.

In this society, today more than ever, what really counts is what everyone owns: power, money, buildings, however, to have all this you need the know-how, namely the ability to conceive, design, build. Possessing, having the know-how does not have much value without integrity and freedom of being.

There are many social mechanisms of slavery, some obvious and easy to identify, others are much subtler and more hidden.

About 45% of the planet's wealth (not just money... but wealth) is in the hands of 280 people (this fact was also reported in national newspapers some time ago and if you consult the relevant lists, you can also find out who the 280 they are). About seven billion people have to live with the rest.

The question that spontaneously arises is: for those who want to be part of this small number of people, which industry or economic sector should they choose?

On reflection, this is the answer I came to:

- The energy sector (including not only oil, but electricity and all derivatives: chemicals, pharmaceuticals, paint, etc.)
- The communications sector (telecommunications, television, etc.)
- The agro-industrial sector

Maybe someone can become one of the wealthiest in some other sector, but these three are the fundamental ones.

As far as the agro-industrial sector is concerned (the concept is also valid for the other sectors) it is not necessary to control the whole chain, just the first stage, i.e. the ownership of the basic genetic material (i.e. the varieties!). Today the best varieties of wheat, soy, tomato etc. are in the domain of multinational companies (who then also control the energy and communications sector). This also explains why these large corporations lose millions of dollars every year in small sectors, such as floriculture, in an attempt to obtain new and better varieties, and they will certainly succeed.

European and national policy-makers cannot escape from the lobbies of these multinationals. We have seen it in telecommunications, the real blocking point that prevented Italy from entering the E.U.: when the telecommunications sector was then liberalised and privatised, the light turned green. This can also be seen in many other sectors, including agriculture: our farmers, floriculturists and nurserymen protest in favour of an E.U. liberal policy towards developing nations. Do you think the owners of the varieties (grown all over the world), of the large distribution chains (which are always the same), really care about this? Whichever way it goes, they always drain the money!

So, it doesn't matter what form of government there is, no matter what the party is and even how good the intentions are, everyone has to deal, more or less openly, with those lobbies.

In Italy, from the post-war period until today, few people have been real revolutionaries or had a long-lasting effect on the country's history. Few of these visionaries had the courage to go against the system and were the architects of the few, still ongoing reforms.

Whoever believes he is free, that he can choose, is in any case a slave to the system.

He is also a slave to communications.

He is also a slave in thought.

Someone may object: *Basically it was always like that, once there were kings...*

One evening, when the Internet first appeared, I was navigating on Gopher (I was surfing more than navigating), from a site in Hong Kong to an Irish site, to another one and so on, until I found it, down there in Florida, an article that caught my attention: How to become rich. I downloaded it and I read all 600 pages of that manual. From that night I could sleep peacefully. For a while I had already suspected that one could not become rich (in the sense of being one of that gang), but from that moment I had an absolute certainty: I could never have been one of them.

That manual was nothing but a modern and up-to-date version, not very good either, of *Il Principe* (The Prince) by Niccolò Machiavelli; anyway, reading it I understood that I could not be someone who was always taking everything from everyone, because in my life I have always done the opposite.

In conclusion we can also ask ourselves: *Okay, suppose that all this is true, what do we do now?*

Do you think with your own head or with one of the media, look at the substance or live your life based on one of appearances?

Icarus wanted to fly and his father, after showing him how to make wings, told him not to fly near to the sun...

But this story then served as a social mechanism for slavery: *Man, stand in your place, don't try to look too high, the heights are not for you, they are for... the leaders.*

In my opinion, Icarus never fell but flew beyond the sun.

The gardens of Lhasa

I keep sleeping but my mind is wandering and leads me to remember ... my first story written in 1994 in the spirit of revenge. The trip to Lhasa had been a destination dreamed of, desired, coveted by the two of us. Then there was betrayal and pain, blind rage and the desire to hurt. This is why I went to Lhasa alone.

What follows is the occasional unconventional report of moments, occurring in more than one space-time *continuum*.

At the Bar Astra 6 (150 parsec from M13)[1] I begin to write what you have already read, but what do you want? These are temporal circumnavigation jokes.

Incidentally, I just saw Andromeda[2] disappear into a black hole but Pier's paintings and Andrea's music[3] have already reminded you of those moments.

If this may appear confusing, it is simply because of your preconceptions, (it happened to me, too); look, on Earth and on many other worlds, you are used to thinking that everything has a beginning, a change and an end, therefore a linear logic derives from it, which necessarily includes time. You could also put the beginning at the end, and vice versa, but the truth could be very, very different.

I leave the tent to watch the morning, the sun at this height is particularly bright and Cri shouts: *Put on your glasses!*

Her smell, after days and days without a bathroom is not good, mine is no better, however the altitude makes it a little more bearable. Early in the morning the air is dry, icy, and cuts your face; I try to look ahead, however the Tsangpo river and Lhasa are not yet in sight. We are going down the road from Shigatse to Gyangtse.

Note

1 - M13 is an agglomeration of galaxies rich in planets. Parsec is a unit of distance used in astronomy equivalent to 3.26 light years (206,205 times the distance of the earth from the sun).

2 - Andromeda, a space ship that, according to legend, carried the best artistic creations of the times, would have disappeared into a black hole... years ago.

3 - Refers to the painter Pier Paderni and musician Andrea Ortu, a notable flutist.

In Tibet *the pan flute, music of the gods* was introduced by the fourth king of the Eight King De Dynasty.

Everest, on the right, is a silent, surreal companion, and all in all indifferent.

I met her at the airport when I knew I would find her, I am aware of this, and I was even then, even if in that space-time *continuum* I did not want to see. Then, the last duel.

The story has to do with the 360-degree reversal of this universe and so the subtle and underhand struggle I was submitted to was:

Do you accept a compromise again?

The compromise of being, doing and having?

And it is on this that the attack came, sudden, brutal, and merciless! An attack of the kind where you no longer know where to turn or hide, and you are huddled in the darkest corner of the stone house, crying.

That attack always comes on several fronts, seemingly they are the physical universe and the other universes that rebel, ally, attract you and then encompass you.

Then, what symbology they assume is another matter, they can be the eyes of another, Israel, a nocturne of Chopin, the blue of an iris, Middle-Earth or something else.

It all starts with one error, then another, then another one and so on and at the end you are asked to accept it and to live without life.

And if you are tempted to have, to do, to be, you are... done!

I knew then — as I know now — that I was going to travel alone to Lhasa, it was unavoidable, but it is sad to lose a traveling companion, to know that for a million years she will still be a slave to her thoughts. But, in the grand scheme of things, what are a few million years? Ethics has the power to erase time, however even now, every now and then, I turn back.

I just left a village after buying bread and cheese, there is also an inn, but I decided on a different night's stay, so I leave behind the dreams perceived so confusingly, some plants on a windowsill, noisy people, cars, yaks and dogs chasing me. (A short time ago Einar[4] brought me a photograph of a similar place to Lhasa and its surroundings.)

4 - Einar Olav Nilssen, Norwegian elf transplanted to Italy and head of Norcom in Milan.

There is a forest in the distance and it is sunset; I go into the vegetation, I choose a clearing under the trees, where I can see the sky. The light filters through the branches and is a magical mix of light and shade. I have always felt fine in the woods, I have never been afraid of its inhabitants, and, inside my sleeping bag, I listen to the night voice, while I look closer and closer at the stars.

I can perceive the life that flows in the trees, and in my drowsiness, I communicate with them, I am one of them, I can imagine the spirits of the woods, the elves, the trolls[5] and other creatures. It is in this area, according to a legend, that the god Avalokitesvara in the form of a monkey and lady Tārā, transformed into a demoness of the rocks, formed the first ancestral couple. I am slipping into dreams and from the depths, the song of Merlin rises lightly to my mind[6]:

Rest you here, enchanter,
while the light fades,
Vision narrows, and the far
Sky-edge is gone with the sun.

Be content with the small spark
Of the coal, the smell
of food, and the breath
of frost beyond the closed door.

Home is here, and familiar things;
A cup, a wooden bowl, a blanket,
prayer, a gift for the god, and sleep.

(And music, says the harp, And music.)

In Norway I met the night and its vitality. In July it is light until 11 p.m. even if it is night, and travelling from Haugesunde to Oslo, I felt and understood it completely. Nature changes, the trees, the

---

5 - Elves and trolls are forest creatures, but while elves are generally good, trolls are often spiteful but not bad. It is believed that the latter are only found in Norway, in fact they can be found in all woods, but they are very difficult to see.
6 - The song of Merlin is taken from *The Last Enchantment* pp. 97-516, by Mary Stewart, Rizzoli 1990.

water in the fjords, the animals, everything tells you that it's night even if there is sunlight like at noon. But, above all, it is the wind that fascinates me, I feel it through the leaves and the fields of barley; it speaks to me sometimes loudly, sometimes in a whisper, I let myself be captured and I no longer have edges, I suddenly find myself smelling junipers, flying on the *médanos*, where the sand flows, until it touches the soul of the whole.

My lips are cracked, my feet are screaming, no rides in the last 20 km, but, at the limit of my vision, trembling, I can finally see Lhasa. The policeman speaks to me in Mandarin, I try to communicate in French, then in English, he does not understand, he nods to me to get on the truck, and that's how I enter the city, near what was once the Western Gate. Lhasa is no longer the ancient Ra-sa — nor the one described by Harrer[7] — but it looks exactly how I imagined it.

The Chinese policemen talk to each other in a language I don't understand, but I know that for them I'm nothing but a nuisance.

The captain speaks in dreadful English, searches my backpack, throwing everything on the table without much regard, looks suspiciously at the Nikon F4 (it is Japanese) and makes me undress. I am completely naked, but the policemen remain impassive, they go over all my things; then the captain looks at my passport.

He does not ask me why I'm there, what I came to do or why I'm not on the tourist circuit. I don't understand what he says, but I guess what is in store for me. He transfers me to a cell, waiting for what the Beijing Intelligence will say, after they, in turn, have checked in Hong Kong.

The door is bolted, it is a sad, naked space, especially because there is nothing of the life that still goes on outside and that, sometimes, we can't resist imagining. The light filters through a small window just to remind me that here the day is ending, the noises of the guests in the next cells, is slowly quietening; only the guard's steps up and down the corridor mark the night. In fact, I could also have chosen another scenario... but that's what I wanted!

I've been here for three days, I act like an ideal guest, I don't protest, I eat even if the food is horrible and I sleep.

---

7 - *Lost Lhasa* by Heinrich Harrer, Harry N. Abrams, Inc. New York, 1992.

Apparently the only one who speaks English is the person I believe to be the captain, and we communicate a little more even if only for a few seconds, especially with our eyes. I feel the answer has arrived, the door opens and a soldier nods to me to follow him.

It's the usual room: all in all, the barracks have the same look, shabby, as the multitude of human beings that inhabit them who don't take care of them; on the walls, besides the dirt, there is coldness and indifference. As in the play *Risciò* when the officer asks the soldier 2777: *You can imagine very well. Who taught you to imagine so well?* and 2777 replies: *Reality, sir.*

The captain is impassive and the question comes dryly: *Why are you here?*
I came to look for the gardens of Lhasa.
The answer leaves him visibly surprised and for a moment his mask falls to let me catch a glimpse of the man.
There are no important gardens in Lhasa and you are my responsibility. Your visa expires in three days; I can keep you in custody or let you go to the hotel, as long as you promise not to cause me problems, that you only go out from morning to sunset and always accompanied by a guide.

He gives me back my things, I don't check right away, but there will be 100 dollars and a pack of cigarettes missing.
I ask him if I can stay in a 'non-western' hotel. His indifferent look seems to tell me: *If it's okay for you...*
A soldier takes me to the Hundred Dragons hotel: it is small, at first sight, there are more or less ten rooms, in fact there are about sixty, leaning against each other with tissue paper walls; the smells of humanity are everywhere, mixed with those of the kitchen and of one-night stands.
The manager, apparently, has already been properly informed, and is also annoyed; we disturbed him while he was busy with a game of *Sho*[9].

---

8 *Risciò: Descrizione di una rivolta*, two-part drama by Angelo Lamberti, from the volume *Teatro* p. 53, Sipario Edizioni, 1993.
9 - *Sho* is a typical Tibetan game that uses wooden balls. It is forbidden for monks.

I put my things on the mat, and I look for the shared bathrooms. The water is cold, slightly reddish; after the shower I don't feel clean, like that time in Sochi[10], but then the dirt was not outside.

At the entrance there is the guide, he seems young, less than thirty years old, and he is obviously Chinese; his name is Huang and something else that I don't understand; he always smiles and speaks good English. I stop listening to him after a minute, even if he goes on undaunted, I wonder how he can talk so much without saying anything. I go out and mix with people. I am not here for the Potala[11] or for Buddhism, however I can't help looking up there, where the symbol defies the blue of the sky.

I think that even that righteous man[12] from 2500 years ago has been completely misrepresented.

I would like to see *Ganden Ngamchö*[13], that is the festival of light, but depending on one's point of view I am either too early or too late.

There is the market in the Barkor[14], I stop by a *Lama Mani*[15] to listen to his story, told with the help of an old *Thangka*[16] greasy and with faded colours. I don't understand what he says, but I follow the sing-song of his voice and the images; there is also a swastika depicted on the Thangka: just think that it has been a symbol of good luck for millennia! Huang would prefer to accompany me to his friends for me to do my shopping, I don't waste time explaining that I leave everything to instinct, and I follow a dark-skinned boy with bright eyes who invites me to see his merchandise: earthenware pots. He

---

10 - Sochi is a city of Georgia.

11 - Potala derives from Sanskrit, in Tibetan its name is Tse, or summit; for others it is the mountain where the god Avalokitesvara, protector of Tibet, resides.
The Potala was built between 1645 and 1694 by the 5th Dalai Lama. It has been the heart of Tibetan civil and religious power for over 300 years.

12 - Siddhartha Gautama Buddha. According to modern scholars, the date of nirvana dates back to 480 BC, according to the Sinhalese tradition in 543 BC; according to the Chinese tradition in 950. In Tibet the birth of the Buddha is placed as being in 1027, 957, 959, 880 or in other dates yet, and nirvana 80 years later. Rolf A. Stein, *The Tibetan civilization*, Giulio Einaudi Editore, 1986.

13 - The *Ganden Ngamchö*, or Festival of Light, takes place in mid-December in honour of Tsong Khapa, the founder of the Gelug order, or Gelugpa, the yellow (reformed) church or the official church of the Dalai and Panchen Lama. During the festival the mountains of Lhasa and surroundings are completely illuminated by a myriad of lights.

14 - Barkor, practically the centre of the city of Lhasa, where a *bazaar market* takes place.

15 - *Lama Mani*, storytellers, beggars and wanderers.

16 - *Thangka*, a silk scroll on which the stories sung by the lama are depicted.

understands that they are not of interest, but he still holds out his hands with a small bowl, the coins disappear in his *ambag*[17] while his mother looks pleased.

I stop by another merchant, and, after intense bargaining – more by gestures than words – I purchase a splendid silk *Katag*[18].

I feel the people's eyes on me, their faces sometimes pale, sometimes burned, the red and orange spots – the monks – but their diffidence is strong: for all of them I am a foreigner.

I invite Huang to an inn, in a corner some patrons are engaged in the 'game of a thousand eyes'[19]; he drinks tea and observes my barley beer, not without a little envy.

Chang evidently considers himself to be working. I leave the centre and head towards the banks of Kyichu[20] where the spirit came to Lhasa from the waters; Huang does not stop talking and follows me continuously. I sit near the water, there are still some women, further down, who finish washing clothes with borax. At the bottom, in the middle there is the *Dzogyab Lukhang*, or the House of the Snake[21], and somewhere, over there, there should be the Oracle of the Rain[22]. Sunset is approaching, the colour and the voice of the water caressed by the willows call me, perhaps to tell the story of this part of the Universe, of the ancient Bod, present-day Tibet, cradle of wisdom, which lost its freedom against the most stupid army in the world. And what was done to Tibet? Violence, killings, deportations.

Nothing new, all in all, in the history of man, even here there is the usual dirty old game, the usual old technique of the illusionist who mixes the cards and confuses them.

17 - *Ambag*, a sort of bag-pouch that the Tibetan merchants wear at the waist.
18 - *Katag*, silk scarves, embroidered or not, particularly symbolic for the Tibetans. When displayed while standing with arms outstretched and hands slightly spaced apart it is a symbol of good luck during a welcome or a farewell.
19 - *Mig-Mag*, Tibetan game. A sort of chess translatable into *the war of a thousand eyes*. It is also generally accepted by the monks. Women prefer the game of *Bagchen* instead.
20 - Kyichu, river near Lhasa. According to the legends, in it lives the Spirit of the Waters.
21 - At the center of the lake is the House of the Snake (Dzongyab Lukhang). The snake is a recurring symbol in many religions.
22 - Oracle of the Rain, the mother was Kiu, half woman and half snake. It is located in Gadong, a monastery near Lhasa.
23 - Point of union. *The teachings of Don Juan. A Yaqui way to knowledge (at the school of the sorcerer)*. (1968), trad. en. by Roberta Garbarini and Tea Pecunia Bassani, Rizzoli, 1999.

And that illusionist is each one of us!

To change the exteriority of things, it would be sufficient to move an anchor point, or the point of union[23] as Carlos Castaneda's Don Juan says, but would I really help myself and these people to have the awareness of Self?

The answer is, obviously, no.

Huang has stopped talking and looks at me thoughtfully; he can't make me out, and this, I assume, leaves him puzzled.

I immerse the bowl in the water, under my touch it feels cold and clean, and I head towards the Potala.

Along the Lingkor[24], a long time ago, in the fourth month (Saga Dawa) the penitents prostrated themselves facing the Potala, but now they do so only as a tourist attraction.

At the beginning of the staircase I hold out my hands carrying the bowl of water; Huang is worried and does not know why. At every step the essence of my being is aroused, it cannot tolerate the void, and tries to fill it using all its strength, all the energy it is capable of. My body is at its limit and I am not yet half way there, I feel time slowing down, approaching zero and mass increasing dramatically step by step. The last tourists who descend are paralysed and unable to move. But I don't allow my mind and thoughts to condition me and, step by step, I move my body up. At the end of the steps there are three of them; more than seeing them, with my eyes full of sweat, I sense them.

The old monk is the wisest, but cannot rebel against his tradition, the second dreams of nirvana, the third is fluid, has no creed and it is towards him that my hands are stretched, it is to him that I deliver the ancient symbol, the ancient awareness. For a moment our human hands touch each other.

I turn and go down the stairs as light as air, Huang this time tells me very seriously that Captain Chen will not be happy with all this; with a shrug I head to the hotel.

---

24 - Lingkor, the bypass of Lhasa and Potala.
25 - The Monastery of Drepung (Depung), about half an hour from Lhasa, at the foot of a mountain, was once the largest in the world. With the monasteries of Sera and Gadong it formed the *three columns* of Tibet.

My dinner is rice, mutton and tea with rancid butter, I go to bed early, bodies are not made to bear all this.

I've just finished breakfast with tea, jam and raisins when Huang arrives, very seriously he informs me that Captain Chen will no longer tolerate any interference or contact with the monks.

It is useless to explain to him that I have done what I had to do; I ask him to see Drepung's monastery[25], he is very suspicious about it, but after half an hour we are on an old bus loaded with tourists from Taiwan.

In the afternoon I decided to visit what was the private garden of the Dalai Lama, in the Norbulingkha, the summer palace that was part of the oracles of the defenders of the faith, and the Garden of the Holy Mother[26].

For the majority of Westerners, they are undoubtedly a disappointment, small spaces, a few plants, some in pots, ragged.

Yet, I feel the love, the passion and the time that has been dedicated to these gardens. I can still perceive the looks full of admiration and concern for these beings who have come from afar. Sitting on a stone I am lost in the history of man and plants, of this vital union between beings so different but so tied to each other and, while I look for a cigarette, I feel in the bottom of my jeans pocket there is something round, which also escaped the search, and which has accompanied me here from my land; it is a cherry stone. I smile to the little clandestine of the worlds and gently entrust it to the earth in a sunny corner of the Garden of the Holy Mother. As I return to the hotel whistling happily, people look at me and smile. Huang is definitely convinced that he is dealing with a complete lunatic. It's my last night in Lhasa, not far from the Inn of the Hundred Dragons there's a disco, it's true that I'm forbidden to go out, but for a moment I don't think about it. Well, if I expected oriental or Tibetan music, this is certainly not the right place, it's only oozing rock, even if tasteless and in the local language.

Between the smoke and the deafening noise I look for a table far

26 - The Holy Mother. In addition to the meanings, easily understood, there is also an important Tibetan woman *the mother* (ma-cig) Labdönma (1055-1145 or 1153) who with Dampa Sangye introduced two important doctrines (zhy-byed and gcod) giving a strong impulse to intellectual activity. Rolf A. Stein, *The Tibetan civilization*, Giulio Einaudi Editore, 1986.

from the dance floor, where men also dance among themselves.
There are several European tourists who stand out like white flies, but they are not very interested in me, some, of course, are looking for girls and ... of course, there are also girls here. The waitress is called Nyima, she is Tibetan but speaks English quite fluently; she has black hair, is not very tall and moves gracefully. I realise that there is a connection between us and I think it would be nice to be able to know her better, but then on reflection I find myself completely in agreement with Ernest[27].

It's time to leave and, after paying the bill, I instinctively take out the Katag bought at the market, I get up and I stretch out my hands towards her; apparently all the Tibetans present understand that gesture. She is undecided and afraid, so I simply say: *Tomorrow I'm leaving, this is the only souvenir I had bought to bring home, but your people, Lhasa's gardens and your smile will be the best memory for me.* At this point Nyima slowly stretches her hands towards the *Katag*. In the disco a round of applause bursts out; I leave without turning back.

At 5.30 a.m. Chen and two helpers knock on the door, enter without any pleasantries and search my backpack for the second time. Expressionless, Chen begins to expose the films, I would like to tell him that I have not taken any pictures but I'm sure he would not believe me.
At the reception the owner is still half asleep, I pay the bill and I get loaded on the truck to the airport. Not a word is spoken during the short trip, I am led to the check-in, then past the metal detector and I wait in the departure lounge. A soldier stays beside me until the last moment; while I'm about to go out onto the tarmac I look up; on the other side, on the balustrade, I see Nyima who holds her hands with a katag towards me, our eyes meet and greet each other for the last time.

The plane to Kathmandu rises from the ground, I look out of the

---

27 - Ernest Hemingway, A *Moveable Feast*, Mondadori, 13th reprint, 1993, pp 41. The passage to which the author refers is the following: *I've seen you, beauty, and now you belong to me, whoever you are waiting for and if I never see you again...*

window, it is dawn in Lhasa. I close my eyes; I review this existence, my last trip. In the Garden of the Holy Mother, in the warmth of the earth caressed by the rising sun, the little clandestine of the worlds is awakening; now I can sleep.

I continue to sleep but my thoughts go far and wide, dwelling on emotional moments in my life. I miss my friend Ezio a lot and whenever I went down to the Riviera I would go to Vallecrosia, simply to have a coffee with him. Our friendship was so deep and disinterested that in the story *A Mar Parà* (Even if everything is going wrong). I mixed his life with mine.

Ezio – *A Mar Parà*

Hi Ezio, what are you doing here? I accompanied you on that last trip from the Sanremo Hospital mortuary to the church in Vallecrosia, and from there to Vallecrosia Alta (The cemetery – Translator Note). You are one of the few who knows all my history and all my contradictions. Without telling you anything, you understood, and you did not say anything, not a word... you simply smiled. You were happy for me, when I visited you with Francesca, I had not yet fully understood how important that woman was to me, you did...
I cannot describe your life, I have to tell mine. I have already mixed yours with mine, and now you are in my current life, alive and present as then. There is no longer any desire for revenge in me, just a little sadness for that girl who lost herself.

This story is dedicated to Ezio, Giuseppe, Giovanni, Giancarlo, Osvaldo, the architect Mario and Giuseppe Balbo, the glorious company *A Mar Parà* and to all those who love flowers and life.
And also for those who don't believe in appearances, either real or imaginary.

The Battle of Flowers in Ventimiglia has deep roots in time and in history; yet it was only officially born on 18 September 1921 and its first rules were written in 1930.
After a ten-year suspension because of the war, it took place uninterruptedly from 1948 until 1969.
There were two further events in 1984 and 1985 and another took place in July 1995.
The Battle of the Flowers developed in a very particular social context.
In those days, the customs and rhythms of life were different from those of today, and many habits of consumer society, especially television, were not yet developed.

The company *A Mar Parà* was set up in 1951 and was perhaps most distinguished by its emblems, creativity and its innovation. All the events told here really happened, only the names of the characters have been changed. In those days the *company*, the design and the creation of floats decorated with flowers was a way of living and dreaming together.

It was also one of the many manifestations of art.

The train finally moved and left Cuneo station. The wooden seat was uncomfortable and it was slippery. The smell of the station was sour, but he did not care. It was holiday time and after long, tedious days he was going to see his home again.

The boarding school was not bad, with its routine, predictable life, but, after a while, boredom together with the desire to escape set in and then without wanting to, his attention wavered from the books for moments on end. At that time, he was not able to control his thoughts, which simply lived their own life and dragged him wherever they wanted.

The old train was panting up through the mountains and the passengers' eyes were lost in the trees, picking up the lights and shadows of the valley.

After a while you got used to the noise and the changes in the light; sensations that disappeared into the back of your consciousness.

The people in the carriage were insipid, empty, watching without seeing. The girl in the corner was not so bad, even if she was playing it cool. His attention shifted to her hips and her legs, too covered up by her skirt. She noticed his look and this embarrassed him. He had not yet been with a girl even if his curiosity was strong.

He closed his eyes and thought back to his first cigarette, secretly smoked with Gianni in the darkest corner of the old cellar; the smoke that escaped towards the light and the smell of tobacco sticking to the walls. When they started to cough and vomit, they rushed to the doorway frightened that someone might see them, but also embarrassed by their weakness.

From there his thoughts turned to the old warehouse on the Aurelia, underground, protected from the light and saturated with the dense humidity of the smell of the flowers.

On the table the flowers were arranged neatly in their boxes; all he could see were his mother's hands working tirelessly.

Vallecrosia in the summer was hot, dry and sunny, very different from Cuneo; the shadows seemed sharper and, in the background, he could hear the quiet murmuring of the sea. In the old attic he had found a chest. Under the neat linen were books left by his uncle, put there when he returned from the seminary and forgotten, perhaps forever. There was the Iliad and the Odyssey, with Latin texts on the opposite page. In the shadow of the attic he met the ancient bards, flying through time; he identified himself with Achilles and with many Gods.

He lived Icarus's adventure of preparing wings for the great challenge, for the flight, right up to the plunge into the void, with his heart screaming in his chest and the blood pressing into his half-closed eyes; then the air returned to fill his lungs and he could see down to the distant earth... he was flying.

It was irrelevant that he missed a page of the book, the last one, he kept flying towards the sun, up, up to Olympus and then even further. That torn page, that unwritten ending, would have affected all his current existence.

He thought about Jan, born in Romania, his companion, friend and teacher. In school they would talk for hours – about philosophy, about their experiences in life. He had not seen him again. He had heard of the disgraceful measures that had been taken against him... just because he had chatted up an 'important' woman. He had gone forever, without even saying goodbye.

He didn't feel resentment for this, he had felt desperation and bitterness, yet distantly, and anyway everything that he had taught him remained, it was his and was part of his being, just like his faith in Icarus, or the pancake tossing on the first evening in school, the hangover after drinking Lluis Maria's sherry, and that oh so sweet look of the drawing mistress as she brushed your head with her hand.

The final train connection for the one going to Albenga, and then his mother's embrace that embarrassed him, as well as the joy emanating from his eyes; he was happy: that evening he would see his friends and sleep within familiar walls to the sound of familiar noises.

Vallecrosia changed its face in summer, the white of the houses was blinding and the blue of the sea was bright and shiny. The first tourists were arriving; at weekends Vallecrosia was transformed and beginning to live faster, though not as much as San Remo, but then the Piedmontese and Milanese tourists were less noisy here.

Flowers were still being sent to Germany and Austria, but the number of boxes was falling daily. The heated fights with flower growers over price, races in the night to the station to load them in time and shipments became a thing of the past. The flower season was coming to an end, the days were longer and his parents were beginning to relax.

Why aren't you going with your cousin Giuseppe? They are preparing the carts for the Battle of Flowers, maybe you can lend them a hand.

His mother was worried about leaving him alone.

Giuseppe was a grown man, and after work he was meeting his friends in the shed behind the laundry. He knew about this new group and had seen the Battle of the Flowers several times, the idea of helping with the construction of the floats was rather appealing to him and then if they were going to win the prize, with his part he could be a little more independent. Anyway it would pass the time.

This was how Giuseppe introduced him into the company.

The first evening he was surprised: in addition to the management team there were also several boys and girls of his age, he knew some of them, who accepted him straight away. Everyone's attention was on the great float project, which in a few weeks would take to the streets of Ventimiglia.

Giuseppe explained the philosophy of the company to him: *A Mar Parà means even if everything is going wrong; what you may not yet understand is the real meaning of 'company': it's very important to build something, to live, rejoice and suffer together, if you win it's even better, if you don't win... no worries, 'A Mar Parà', even if everything is going wrong, you still get a dinner out of it and then there will be another chance.*

He worked with the others for several nights, between one bottle of wine and the next, between spaghetti dinners and laughs; at the end, his hands hurt, and he had lost count of the carnations and the sempervivens he had nailed and glued.

On the last night, only a few of them went back home, and then just to change.

In the morning the roar of the tractor and the huge float appeared on the road, on display to the people.

It was very heavy and the wheels left their mark on the asphalt that was starting to melt. The float was creaking and even if the noise was hidden by the tractor and the people's applause, the controllers were following every single vibration, they would look each other in the eyes: *One kilometre to go, we should make it.* Metre by metre, applause after applause, they were keeping an eye on the girls on the *Goddess of Flowers* float, who smiled and smiled, ready however to jump down at every sign of collapse. At the finish line the tension suddenly relaxed. You could finally let out the screams, the hugs, the pats on the shoulders, the *We did it!*

The sun quickly dried the cold sweat of fear.

No, they did not win. They only came seventh. Too bad, the *Goddess of Flowers* float had seemed to him the most beautiful in the world, but... next year. They were already looking forward to the next challenge, to the next adventure. They had dinner anyway, some obviously not in agreement with the jury's verdict, however to come seventh, out of at least thirty competitors, was already a great success. Giuseppe, the engineer, and Mario were already thinking about the next theme.

He only had eyes for Maria, who was a few years older, and was much more experienced. After dinner he took her home, hand in hand, his desire increasing step by step. In the street's darkest corner, their instincts would prevail over shyness and shame. He simply did not think anymore, the taste of her lips, the first kiss, left him surprised; then his hands became audacious, first insecure and then frantic under her skirt. Staring off into the darkness, he tried to relive what had just happened, so quickly, against a tree, under the stars. The surprise of her body, the frantic and uncontrolled movement, the shock he tried to stop, the embarrassment of letting go and a part of him that, in his inner depths, remained indifferent and that he could not define.

His return to boarding school came with a mixture of feelings: on the one hand the sadness of leaving his home and on the other the joy of seeing his friends after the holidays. He did not relate anything about that summer except for his entrance into the floats' company, and that when school finished he would have a car.

He was learning quickly and did not need to study much, at least the subjects he liked.

It would take him many years to fully understand the reasons for this. During the lessons that interested him he was simply observing, this was accompanied by his total attention and presence.

The following year, on the first of June, *A Mar Parà* came second with *Flowers and Fountains* and the following one with *The Firebird*. It was a strange feeling leaving school for the last time, to a certain extent it meant leaving the certainty and routine of a life programmed by someone else, but on the other hand he had the whole world to discover and... *A Mar Parà*.

He arrived at the shed that evening with the '600' station wagon, used in the company to transport the flowers.

The engineer's problem was the usual, the floats were heavy and a supporting structure, steering and solid, and resistant wheels were needed: *Like those of a tank;* the engineer nodded: *Exactly!*

The next day they were on their way to Turin. They had heard that there was a place where they demolished army surplus material.

As they wandered between old military trucks and steel carcasses, they thought of the terror and slavery that they had led to, but in the end they had also brought the dream of freedom. Symbols: symbols of insanity and degradation of being.

The way back seemed shorter to him. He did not even notice the mountains as he was so excited, they had the strongest wheels in the world for their float, the theme remained to be decided.

In a moment of quietness, he spoke to his friends about the feelings he felt when he saw those rusty steel monsters, the hopes and dreams of those who had left and those who had remained.

Someone suggested timidly: *Why don't we build the Dream Carriage?* Quietly they thought about this, and at last Giuseppe said: *Dreaming is the sugar of life, it is what allows us to continue to hope, it is an open door in time. If you all agree, then we can do that. The Dream Carriage it is.*

That evening, while Giuseppe and the Engineer were projecting and designing the frame, he and Antonio went to Gianni's butcher shop in the '600'. Gianni, another member of the company, had collected all the bulls' balls from the various slaughterhouses.

They were in cold storage, three full bags! But... how many bulls had they killed? Nobody took the trouble to count how many testicles there were. The red wine, the fire grilling them till late at night; he slept in the shed with the most of the others from the company.

Spring was late, it had been cold and rainy; on 23 May the mayor of Ventimiglia issued the order to move the Battle of the Flowers to 13 June. This news caused heated discussion, some were in favour and some were against; Giuseppe cut it short: *It's better, this gives us more time to prepare the Dream Carriage*. The metal framework occupied almost the entire shed, they began to apply the papier-mâché and the moss, to form the dream and the two gigantic, multi-coloured snails that would drive it.

On the morning of 13 June, there was a warm breeze, the sun was beginning to brighten hopes. They quickly moved the shed wall, the tractor began to grumble and the *Dream Carriage* offered itself to the light of day and the waiting people.

The girls with long white dresses and flowers in their hair took their places. The float was heavy but they were counting on the solidity of the tanks' wheels marking the asphalt on the Aurelia.

Paris was not like London, serious and muffled, yet in its own way fascinating. In Paris the sun was more alive, people were more cheerful and always smiling, Paris really was a Moving Feast. And so the next year, he simply said: *Paris Pigalle;* it came out almost without thinking.

The idea is great, what's not so great is that it's impossible to achieve: how do you represent Pigalle? Paolino's intervention, so sudden, shifted the company's attention to the impossible challenge; the problem was no longer the subject, but how to achieve it: *There is nothing impossible for A Mar Parà, we can do it, even the impossible.*

Giuseppe and the Engineer were already working out the design of the float.

The Moulin Rouge is fine, the streetlights, the lamps, but the problem is the costumes: where are we going to get the costumes for the girls?

Eh, smart guy! We can't go and rent them in Paris.

This problem stopped him for a week, then the idea came, maybe a crazy one: what did they have to lose? He and Claudio, went to Nice that afternoon. *What put such a thing in your mind? I think the bouncers will send us away with a kick up the ass.*

Why should they? he replied: *In Nice there are places where they do cabaret and striptease, we go in and ask them where they get the girls' clothes, that's all.*

Monsieur Jean, as he was known, was kind to them, he knew the Battle of the Flowers. Unfortunately, he did not know where the girls got their clothes, but if they stayed for the show they could ask them directly.

Valérie, that was her stage name, had the ability to transform herself. On the stage, in swirls of smoke, lights and sounds she was completely different from the person before them. And yet she was the queen of the French Riviera. When he explained the reasons for their presence, she burst out laughing and called over the others: *D'accord alors, c'est Madame Zais.*

His companion remained silent all the way to Monaco, then he spat it out: *Why did you say yes?* And again: *Belin* (typical Ligurian form of address), *who is going to tell our girls that we're putting the French girls on the wagon?*

In practice they had agreed the following: the name and address of the seamstress who made the costumes in exchange for their presence on the wagon; this way, not only were they going to the Battle of Flowers for free and in the forefront, but they were going to live it as protagonists.

As our carriage represents Pigalle, even the girls must be French, is it clear? The look that anticipated the answer was: *Maybe, but I think you want to take the brunette to bed.*

They went often to Madame Zais in Nice, officially to chose and try on clothes.

In mid-May an article appeared in the Secolo XIX newspaper: it anticipated how exceptional their float would be; less than a week later, the Village Gauls replied that: *This time, A Mar Parà has found someone who really knows a lot about floats.*

Giuseppe was agitated; the Engineer too: *I don't care if Barbadirame*

(Copperbeard) is working for the Galli bordigotti (The Gauls of Bordighera), our float is the nicest, and then we have... the French chicks.

The girls, led by Valérie, arrived on the evening of 3 June. When they saw the float where they were arranging the last flowers, they were amazed. The shed was lit up. *Paris Pigalle* in the centre of people running about all over the place, arranging heads the heads of carnations and sempervivens, electricians struggling with the latest light bulbs and huge batteries. *C'est fantastique!, c'est incroyable!*

Valérie had wet eyes and a trembling voice: *Mon Dieu, et... et... vous avez fait tout ça pour un seul jour... you did all this just for one day, but what am I saying, one day, just for an hour, for ten minutes?*

Paolino arrived breathless: *They are saying all kind of things, A Mar Parà is in trouble as the float cannot pass through the streets because of badly parked cars; and there's also someone who's saying that A Mar Parà hasn't made it because the tractor driver is a man from the Galli* (Gauls) *who will do everything to delay the departure.*

The truth was that after just a few metres, with the weight of paper and wet moss, flowers, light bulbs and a few tons of batteries under the floorboards, the cart had split an axle.

For over an hour they worked like crazy, not giving a damn about their new clothes, their hands bleeding; then at last... on the front, the baby girls, then the little bombers that would bombard the crowd with flowers and at last *Paris Pigalle*, moving towards its destiny... *Go, for God's sake... go! Paris Pigalle* arrived just a few minutes before the competition's closing signal. Despite the applause, the throwing of flowers, the costumes, Valérie's emotion and the French girls' smiles, the float was disqualified.

The following year, with *Of loves and ladies, knights and arms, A Mar Parà* came second. The company challenged the jury: the carriages are made for the eyes of the people – the light, the colours, the shapes, the movements should not be judged in a shed!

Sanremo is important, the Sanremo Festival is something that Italians watch with passion, and no one has yet used it as a theme for their float; there are songs like Quando... Quando... Quando... (When... When... When...) *that did not win but they are going all around the world...*

They were all dismayed, speechless... the heads of their figurines had been stolen. *It was the 'Gauls of Bordighera', I'm sure they did it!*
It probably is but no one saw them ... Let's go and give them a lesson ... We all agree to make a complaint to the carabinieri against persons unknown, but now ... now what are we going to do?
Stop it guys, while you are moaning about this, nothing is getting done; our artist can redo the heads, it means that we will have to work harder, I tell you that we can and must do this.
It was the turn of the Gauls to be disqualified for irregularities, as their *Don Quixote* was higher than the regulation, and *A Mar Parà* was first with *The Song Festival 1963*.

That year he met someone who was to be important to him. Later he will have children and he will feel a little bit like God. Even later he will fully and totally understand that the distance between two people cannot be measured by the metre.
Leave me alone, don't bother me, and let me smoke in peace.
That morning he was quiet, he knew he was going to meet her, he knew it the moment he opened the door to leave the house. He knew it when he first looked in her eyes, and, despite his smiles, he felt a sweet sadness and melancholy.
She smiled, in her black dress with her breasts free under the fabric, she was occupying his space; the physical contact, the caresses in the taxi, the key turned to show the number of her room.
He looked at himself in the mirror and said: *Go ahead but remember that you will get into trouble.* He discovered her body and part of his dreams, the sweetest moment was when he gave her an iris, blue as the sky and as hope.
Bellagio, Milan, Sanremo, Treviso, Padua, Trapani and Messina... Saint Paul de Vence to buy signs, Nice ... a unique universe in Baia Benjamin... Tarquinia... moments that burned quickly but how lovely it all was. Between one kiss and the next: *Never put me in front of faits accomplis, remember, I want to be your friend even after... love can pass... friendship never!*
Maybe she had not heard, maybe she had forgotten, maybe she didn't understand. That, for him had been a declaration of love and surrender, giving free rein to his interiority, every protection and barrier removed.

With his eyes fixed on the darkness and a sense of prostration, he dreamed of hitting the ground, before him a black, terrifying mass. As he watched, it disappeared, leaving him with a feeling of discomfort. He thought to himself: *Is it possible that the symbols of religion are so powerful?*

In front of him two doors, one pink and one blue, the feeling of mystery, the invitation to choose, to discover... He had the exact perception of the trap, of the story that repeats itself, of being starved by being. No, he was not going to exchange ethics with having.

Nobody had the power to convince him that Icarus had fallen... he turned his back and went away...

The next day, on the phone, he told her: *You have lost me...!*

From a false and remote distance, he got: *No, I have not lost you.*

The golden lake, the flight of moths, the blue of the iris: they were no longer there. What remained was the greyness and solidity of a lost being.

What are you looking at, what do you find so interesting?

I'm looking at this valley, the flowers, the fields, the cherry trees, I look at them closely because I will never see them again.

No one can teach another person to fly... if he does not want to, just as no one can teach anyone self-respect and life. He taught his children that everyone is free without any limits... even to choose slavery.

In 1964 Osvaldo designed a true masterpiece: *The dream of a prisoner.* What does a prisoner really dream about? Freedom, women, wealth, power, immortality, flying or... simply what was there before!

We don't have to build the whole body, the head is enough if it is expressive... The problem is the weight...

A carriage is made up of a frame, papier-mâché, wet moss, flowers, decorations... It's impossible...

No, nothing is impossible, we just have to find the solution, but if we don't look for it we'll never find it!

Did you see on the television show 'Campanile Sera', they showed a new material that is very light and can be easily shaped just as you want...

Call the National Television RAI and see where they make that stuff.

For three cubic metres of polystyrene, it took a truck, high volume and low weight, one problem was solved but another was there, and not unimportant.

So, what do we do now? The polystyrene can be sculpted and shaped and it's light, but it doesn't absorb water, so what do we do about the flowers; if the polystyrene does not absorb water, after one night they will be dry and dead! Well, if we cover the polystyrene with wet newspapers, maybe we can do it...

He had been struck by lightning, he was still alive, he had felt the energy, huge, alien and... cold, crossing him. The attack had been cruel, brutal and from multiple universes at the same time. He was floating on the floor, out of his body, thinking about the immensity of the worlds, yet discovering them... small, cruel and limited.

He had made his choice... but the voice of the one who had loved the most was lost in humanity. Poor prisoner, it is not the blindfold on your eyes that takes away the light, and it is not the bars of the cell or the limits of the body that keep you from flying. His thoughts were interrupted by the announcement: *The Prisoner's Dream* with 94.6 points is the WINNER... *A Mar Parà* won again with *The Chinese Fairy Tale, The Sabbath of the Witches* and *Baron Münchhausen*; in 1968 and 1969 it came second with *The God of the Sea* and with *La corrida*. In 1984 the companies were recreated, *A Mar Parà* with *Carnival in Rio* reaching fourth and in 1985 *The Great Gatsby* came second.

I return from my trip to the Riviera, I feel strange, I perceive the presences that are with me along the way, I believe I can see them, but no it is not possible, I look more carefully towards the sea... and yet... now I also feel the voices, the cheers of enthusiasm, I see the baby girls who carry the letters that make up the name of the company, *A Mar Parà*! The bombers throwing flowers and... here... the float... but... this time Ezio chose... the flight of Icarus... back then, he never believed the last page... but it is him driving and... he is flying... flying towards the setting sun.

But Ezio, then you did all this just for one day, but what am I saying, one day, just for an hour, for ten minutes...

Knowledge and prejudices

I'm sleeping, but my thoughts are awake, they are changing all the time; I am passing willy-nilly from memories to what I believe to be the present. Suddenly I find myself in Sicily where I accidentally meet a man who tells me how he started working with puppets.

He proudly shows me his creatures, their movements. I am attracted to the bright colours and by his pride in them, but also by his sadness and melancholy. Now puppets are no longer so popular.

He had hoped to be able to pass on his knowledge to someone else; he was bitter that all his experience would be lost.

He had no children, only an assistant apprentice, perhaps he didn't have much imagination, but... he knew how to draw and make the puppets... maybe... maybe his story would have a tomorrow.

He must leave me as his show is about to start...

I open my eyes and find myself at the hospital, however my bed is boxed in by screens, like in a Japanese house; on the left there is a shadow that resembles Mickey Mouse's head, serious, it's not moving. I wonder what this means, I have the impression that I hear the voice of Katrin ordering me to: *Reflect on your last experience, reflect and when you have the solution press the button that is by your side.*

I look to my right and actually a two-button device is hanging there, one green button and one red; I think about it a lot, I reconsider the discussions with Katrin, my stories, Barcelona, New York, Lhasa, Ezio, Sicily... and my thoughts; then I press the green button, and after a few minutes I see a shape behind the screen.

A voice that I assume to be Katrin's says: *Tell me.*

Knowledge is good for everyone and therefore collective, cannot be individual and our purpose and goal are to share all our experiences, everything we know, without alteration, and in the most honest possible way to others.

I close my eyes, when I re-open them the screens have disappeared and the room is back to normal. Katrin arrives with a nurse, they discuss the therapy; she looks at me, but says nothing about the answer to my question.

A few days later, I discuss with Katrin what has happened to me and the possible causes. She explains that the origins of heart disease are different, and that in my case they depended on predisposition and lifestyle; cigarettes may have accelerated the problem but were not the main cause. Katrin goes on to explain that another cause for heart problems are modified HIV virus strains. The phenomenon is common, especially in the homosexual community, but it is spreading rapidly also among heterosexuals. I think out loud and I tell her that I don't very much like the world of seropositives and homosexuals. Katrin goes away and I go to sleep. When I open my eyes, the screens are there again, I'm boxed in once more; I turn around and see the old image of Mickey Mouse's head against the light. This time Katrin does not speak, I assume that she is somewhere in the back. I say to myself: *If the method of last time is valid, what is the problem that needs solving? What did we talk about, did I say something wrong?* Mentally, I recall the meeting with Katrin, I reflect on what we said and suddenly... I think I understand. I push the green button and, without waiting for anyone, I speak out loud: *We need to pay close attention to prejudices. All people are sacred, and no one has the right to judge. People are not stupid, they commit stupid actions, and that is very different.*

Bergamo

I live in a sort of limbo, I hear distant voices, but I cannot see anything. *Mr. Croci, you are at the Ospedali Riuniti of Bergamo, you had a serious problem with your aorta, which is the main artery in the body, but now everything is fine.*

I am totally confused, I was in Barcelona, how did I end up in Bergamo?

I still can't see anything, I'm always in a muffled universe and faraway I hear voices, maybe doctors in discussion, I don't understand what they are saying, but I see a computer image of an aorta. Where it branches it is possible to see the split, and a voice says: *Here, the problem has arisen here, the genetic breakage occurred here.* I don't understand what that means.

The voices start again, it's my wife's, her tone is altered: *I knew it, I imagined it, who knows how many women he has been with, he made me ill too.* Someone else answers, *No madam, you are perfectly healthy, you have never been infected.*

My friend Franco Locatelli is close to me, I don't see him clearly, I can hardly see him, he speaks to me and says; *Don't worry, now everything is fine, I will speak with Gina and I will explain to her that things are not like that.*

I don't understand anything anymore, I don't know what he is talking about.

The voices continue: *Mrs Carnelutti showed up here after she had heard what happened, she wanted to keep the strictest secrecy, in the past she has had relations with the patient, however from the tests it does not look as though she is infected.*

I am increasingly confused, I was in Barcelona, now in Bergamo; what is happening, I just don't know.

Here is another voice, it is Francesca, from what I understand she is with her husband and talking to the doctors, perhaps... *Madam, the strain that we isolated from you corresponds perfectly with Mr Croci's... And also corresponds to that of the Mr CR you indicated. He passed away two years ago; we asked the hospital and the data we received match, apparently the cycle of infections in that strain of the virus is only between Mr CR, you and Mr Croci.* I hear a voice that I don't recognise, but I understand to be that of Francesca's husband: *This is what you did, and now it's clear why you were always going out...*

I don't want to have anything to do with you anymore... we will go our separate ways... and just to be clear, the children will stay with me...

I am sad for Francesca, I make a tremendous effort, but no word comes out of my mouth, even if my mind is doing everything to defend her.

Another voice says: *There is also the problem of biological damage to Mr. Croci.* The answer from the man who is surely Francesca's husband: *I am a man of honour, if I have to answer for damages, my insurance also covers damages caused by my wife.*

I don't understand, I close my eyes and sink into darkness.

Katrin is leaning over and looking at me, now my confusion is total, however she explains: *Our experimental group, which you met in Barcelona, was partly dismantled: Giovanna and I ended up in Bergamo, at the Halls Foundation, others remained in Barcelona or returned to their respective countries. You were cured of your heart problem, but we also knew you were a carrier of a modified HIV strain; and that in the long run it could give you problems - and so it was. You had a dissecting aneurysm of the aorta, the surgeons implanted a prosthesis, but you had a blockage in the blood vessels in your left leg and now we are curing you.*

I hear the voice of my wife, of Francesca, of her husband, far away. I am mixing everything together.

Treatments with flow machines, electrostimulations, physiotherapy, I can't feel my left leg any more, and despite all my efforts it doesn't move a millimetre.

I hear a distant voice, I recognise it, it's that of my niece Elena: *My aunt isn't bad, she's just a bit stubborn...* I can't hear the rest, and I cannot even understand the meaning of what I did hear.

Now it is my wife who speaks: *You'll soon be able to go home...*

Heart and reason

I find myself in isolation again with the screen that hides the outside world, the icon of Mickey Mouse on the right, but strangely this time Katrin is next to me, on the side of my bed. She looks at me and says very seriously: *This time the problem's more difficult, you are faced with two choices, both logical, both valid; one involves the mind and the other the heart... I refer to your wife and Francesca.* I answer: *My wife's waited for me, she's made a lot of sacrifices for me.*

Katrin remains silent for a moment then mutters: *It is logical, I understand, but for once I would have preferred the heart to win.*

You know I love her, but she has infected me.

Francesca was honest with you, she told you her story right away, she loves you, and then this is a unique chance you have of living with her, then it will be too late, and you will lose her forever.

I reflect, close my eyes, place my hand on my chest and: *I choose... the heart.*

Later I tell my wife: *I will not go home with you, I want to leave because I love someone else and I want to live with her for the rest of my time.*

It's dark, or maybe it's me who is not seeing; I hear voices, my wife

is saying: *I knew he had someone else.* Franco Locatelli: *No, don't worry, I'll try to make him think this over, you'll see that everything will be fine.*
Dr. Abele: *He's a fool, how can he possibly leave his wife, a saint of a woman for the one who infected him with HIV.*
Gina: *If that's his choice then so be it, but he will have to pay very dearly for the time I've devoted to him.*

The Foundation is preparing for the big party on 6 January.
The grand palace is tidied up in order to accommodate the important good citizens of Bergamo, as well as from the neighbouring cities, more than a thousand people and the television broadcasters; the party is mainly organised to raise funds and the charity evening is organised with this aim. Katrin and the rest of her team are busy with the preparations and I see little of her. Nurses come regularly into my hospital room, but doctors only occasionally.
I begin to understand how it works, the one who gives the orders is the President, but his wife, daughter and sister are very influential, and it is through them that Katrin manages to get everything she wants. I also understand that my doctor is cheating a bit, she is equipped with the oddest electronic devices and in practice she is spying, listening almost permanently to everything that is said in the corridors of power.

I open my eyes, then close them and open them again, and I say: *It's not possible*, and yet Francesca is here, I recognise her behind the mask, she realises I'm awake and she smiles; her *Hi*, penetrating deep in my consciousness and in my heart. *How is it possible that you're here and then how... as a nurse?*
Do you remember when I told you that I had attended courses? Luckily, I did them all, and even though I'm just a hospital assistant, this has allowed me to work here as a volunteer and to be near you.
Actually, your doctor, Katrin, has also helped me.
I hold her hand for a long moment until she says: *Now I have to go.*
The following day Katrin explains: *All the important good people of Bergamo will be at this big party on the sixth, everyone wants to show off; that's why we are busy organising different events that, in one way or another, will raise funds for the foundation.*

She keeps on smiling: *I have a big surprise in store for you and Francesca, concerning the fact that you are now practically free, so you can marry, at least civilly. The marriage could be publicly celebrated by the President of the foundation on 6 January. The fact that a patient treated by a foundation hospital and in the process of being cured is getting married in public is positive and important news for the media and besides, people like a public marriage, at least if it's well orchestrated. Are you willing to show off?*
Before I say yes, I would like to know if Francesca agrees.
She smiles beguilingly: *Certainly she agrees, otherwise I wouldn't even have spoken to you.*
Well, then it's okay for me too.

I wait for Francesca to arrive, the marriage plan proposed by Katrin leaves me pleasantly surprised. Marriage for me is not compulsory, in the sense that loving Francesca I feel already tied to her for life, but if she likes... Finally, the door opens, and she enters, dressed in gown and mask, I take off her mask, stroke her hair and brush her lips first with my fingers and then with my mouth.
The big day is approaching, Katrin is very busy with the organisation, and Francesca gets to see me as often as possible.
For new year's eve, the Foundation has organised a charity raffle, at midnight the first prize ticket will be selected: a Fiat Lancia; Katrin insists that Francesca buys at least one raffle ticket. Francesca gives her ten euros saying: *Well... you never know.* Katrin tears off the ticket and winks.

Midnight approaches, Francesca and I follow the live broadcast from the Foundation's tower, without any interest; there are interviews, short documentaries on how the foundation operates, announcement of the minor prizes. We wait for the new year talking about events that come to mind, casually, and about what it would be nice to do together in the future; the images on the screen follow each other and finally the announcement of the final prize takes place; in that moment we are seeing in the new year with a kiss, when we open our eyes, the winning ticket number is displayed on the screen; Francesca says: *Let me check.* She puts her hand into her purse, pulls out the ticket and, after checking, says amazed: *It's mine... it's not possible, please check it too.* The serial number is really hers, in my mind's eye I see Katrin winking, and I think to myself: *How did she do this?*

Go, run, they are waiting for you.. Francesca laughs like a child, adjusts her skirt, combs her hair and goes out... I wait and, after a while, she is on the video with her beguiling smile that gets me every time; it is a moment of joy and at the awarding of the prize her thank you radiates everywhere.

In my drowsiness I record my wife's presence, her voice is full of resentment and hard feelings, I understand only a few words... and all for that one there, on television... even if I have granted the separation, he will not get rid of me so easily... he will have to pay... Yeah, I think, paying... as if everything was for sale, as if everything could be bought... can love and life be bought?

The wedding is scheduled for the evening of 6 January. Katrin and PR study the best way to promote the event and at the same time try to find a solution so that, since I'm immobilised in bed, I don't come into direct contact with the media. The ceremony will be simple, the wedding will be celebrated by the Foundation President; the President's daughter and Katrin will be the witnesses.

Everything follows as if in a dream, the moment arrives; Francesca makes her entrance wearing a very simple cream suit, I get lost in her eyes. Everything takes place far away, in a muffled environment, my attention is all on her; I hear a voice speaking, rings appear, she thought of it, and it is... YES.

The cameras flashing are endless, the photographers record second after second, there is nothing they can miss and yet, inside of me and inside Francesca, what we say with our eyes, with the touching of our hands, is only ours.

I cannot move out of bed, but Francesca leaves me to go to the tower with the President for the television transmission and to show herself to the guests; this is not making me very happy, but I cannot help it. Katrin can read me and says: *Don't worry, I'll bring her back as soon as possible, and then I'll try to give you some intimacy.*

I cannot help but wait, from the bed I follow what happens on the live television broadcast, seen this way Francesca looks even more beautiful. Here she is, finally. The propaganda campaign is over, she runs up and hugs me. Katrin and her assistant also enter the room, she looks at us smiling and says: *For your first night we have found an isolated room, no microphones or cameras, it's downstairs.* After saying this she unlocks the bed and with the help of her assistant pushes it towards the door and to the lift. She says: *We have to hurry up, before anyone sees us, the paparazzi are desperate to know where you are.* The lift goes down one level, Francesca next to me. The room on our first night is a common hospital room, with a bed, a television and a window that overlooks somewhere. Katrin and her assistant place my bed next to the other. *I'm sorry,* says Katrin, *unfortunately we don't have a double bed.* Francesca, smiling, says: *It will be enough.* Katrin and the assistant go out saying: *Leave the key in the lock, this will prevent anyone from opening the door, even with the master key.*

We are alone, Francesca gives me a kiss, then quickly, without taking her eyes off mine, begins to undress. I'm excited, I take off my shirt, with the healthy leg I push down my pants and laboriously I succeed to take them off. Her body is on mine, my skin in contact with her. Her lips slide down my body, they seek me, encompass me, my fingers make their way into the folds of her skin; my excitement grows until I come: she moves up, her mouth merges with mine, our tongues play, oh yes, they intertwine and chase each other. She breaks away for a moment and pulls out from her bag a little box with a condom, smiling she puts it on me: *It's the first time we'll have done it with a condom, the doctors want this, even if now I don't think it's necessary, as we are both HIV-positive and you cannot have children.* She is above me, but I don't feel her weight, she lifts her pelvis for a moment and we become a single being, our lips are seeking each other, as are our hands, our breath accelerates and melts, her body starts to tremble, our hands tighten spasmodically, then, slowly, the sea of emotions is subsiding, and the sweat begins to cool on our skin. With one hand I cover our bodies with the sheet; I *don't want to sleep, I want to look at you, be sure you're here... I don't want to wake up from this dream...*
She looks at me gently, puts a finger on my lips and kisses my eyes. We stay like that, hugging each other until sleep comes. But even in sleep the hug continues and my soul is finally at peace.

We wake up almost at the same time, our lips, slightly dry, are looking for each other, we savour the taste of our mouths, we are searching each other with our hands, with our skin, with our eyes: *I have to go, it's already very late.*
She gets up and goes to the bathroom.

Someone knocks lightly but firmly on the door, Francesca looks out, covered by a towel and opens the door; Katrin enters, followed by a nurse. *Hello guys, I hope your first night was nice.* I reply: *Yes, Katrin, mainly thanks to you.* Francesca gives me a kiss while they push my bed to the door, her skin is fresh: *See you later,* and our eyes chase each other.
I am back in my room, the physiotherapist has manipulated my leg, and treated the bed sores on my heels, on my sacrum and on my head. In my drowsiness I hear voices in the next room: *Don't think that I am leaving like this, I've been his servant for a lifetime...*
It's Gina and I don't know who she is talking to, however her thoughts are very clear.

I think about possible solutions for my ex-wife but it's complicated; practically I don't own anything, and I'm immobilised in bed.
In the afternoon, I talk about the problem with Francesca and she thinks about it, then says: *What would you say if we offer her the car, it's new, it would be useful for getting me to work, but the old one still works very well. I'm sorry, you won that car...*
It's not important, I told you, we'll buy another one when we can.
When we inform Katrin about the matter, she turns her nose up: *I wouldn't give her anything, if she wants she can sue, do whatever she wants, she won't be able to win anyway, if you two feel like you want to be charitable, I recommend you get the Foundation's lawyer to conduct the negotiations: he is paid specifically to do this job. Whatever you do, you absolutely must avoid direct contact with the lady. In addition, the lawyer will sort out the compensation for biological damage against Francesca's ex-husband; this is easier because the Managers' Health Insurance has excellent cover and has to pay out...*

Katrin leaves us with the commitment to inform the lawyer to bring our offer to my ex-wife.

She replied that this isn't enough, even if she can't drive the car, okay, she considers it a down payment, but it isn't adequate.

The lawyer is at the foot of my bed. I ask him to leave me some time to talk with Francesca.

I could ask an uncle of mine, he will certainly answer no, but my aunt could convince him, it would be a loan and we will return the money when we can.

Francesca, I don't know what to do, my accounts are blocked, my business has stopped. I am immobilised in bed, however sooner or later I will be able to return to work...

Francesca: *I'm going to talk to Katrin and phone my aunt to see if we can arrange a visit during one of the next weekends.*

Francesca returns after an hour with a radiant air: *All right, next Saturday we will go to Modena, Katrin will come too with a group of nurses by motorbike. I didn't know she liked bikes so much, for you they will organise transport with a sidecar.* I don't mind, I have been stuck in the hospital for many months and an excursion to the old Emilia attracts me, I would like to pay a visit to my house, but I understand that I can't ask for everything.

The moment of departure arrives, getting into the sidecar with my leg in a brace is quite complicated. I am finally seated even though, thanks to the partial insensitivity of my left bottom cheek, the seat isn't very comfortable. The engine is started, and we slowly get going. Through the plexiglass of the helmet, I notice that the road is narrowing as we increase speed. While the air rushes against my face, my thoughts are lost in a thousand streams, trying to build an ideal scene, a potential future; so, without realising that time is passing, we arrive at the Modena motorway exit, 20 minutes more and we will reach our destination.

The bikes, one after the other, enter the courtyard of Francesca's uncle's country house. I am a little embarrassed by the noisy motorcycles, the renovated farmhouse suggests to me another space, another time. Finally, the engines stop and the atmosphere slowly returns to its original state.

While they greet us, I examine their faces, they are both simple people, she and him, used to acting on instinct, and a sort of cautious fatalism gained from hard work in the fields and with age that advances relentlessly. I realise that their eyes are focused with greater curiosity on me, their words are polite but they look as if they are trying to work me out. From the movement of their eyes and the relaxation of their faces, I assume that the judgment is quite positive, even if clearly provisional.

The table is prepared outdoors, those who aren't helping are wandering around; I do too, even if I cannot go too far from the courtyard in the wheelchair. Lunch sends me back in time, it has been many years since I have eaten *anolini in brodo*, also the taste of beef and *salamella* is unique; after a few bites the buzz of the diners is fading, and I find myself travelling back in time.

I go back to Case Levori, where I was born. I relive the wedding lunches or the feast days in the room in the house where I was born; that room was not big but then, with the eyes of a child, it seemed huge. Right there, Francesca and I made love to each other, standing on the ground, intensely and furiously. Now that house has collapsed; after the division of my grandfather's estate, that house was given to my Uncle Luigi, and his sons had other interests than to renovate an old house in the mountains. I cannot blame them too much; they were born and raised in London; in Castelletto they already had another apartment, so why worry about it.

The smell of coffee brings me back to the present, Katrin hands me my dose of pills that I swallow before the slice of cake; the diners begin to get up and walk around the town. I stay in the courtyard, in the sun, the girls and Francesca help to clear and tidy up.
It's time for goodbyes, a handshake for Francesca's uncle and a kiss on the cheek for her aunt, I think their judgment of me is positive. Francesca has not yet informed me about what they said in private but from how she smiles I understand that the answer is positive, before leaving she whispers that they will make the loan, we will give them back the money when we can.
I settle in the sidecar, the engines rumble and with a wave of the hand we are moving towards the highway, I turn and see the house and that time is moving away quickly.

The lawyer shakes his head: *No, Arturo, your ex-wife does not accept the car and the 14,000 euros you propose. I met her yesterday, she came to my office with her brother. Basically, what you agreed in words is no longer valid, she continues to repeat hysterically that you must pay, but it's impossible to understand how much or how. She is also threatening to sue the President of the Foundation.*

At that point, the lawyer informs us that the legal action against Francesca's ex-husband could provide enough money and at this stage liquidating my ex-wife could be easier. I say to the lawyer that I have to reflect on the situation. I actually want to talk to Francesca in order to find a solution on which she agrees.

When the lawyer goes out, Francesca and I look at each other, she says: *There's another problem: if you sue my ex-husband, the insurance will certainly pay, but then they will no longer accept him as a client; so my children will have no cover.*

We are grasping at straws, so I say, with a peck on her cheek: *I'll tell the lawyer to give her the 14,000 euros in advance and to be patient, I will find more money... we'll find a solution.*

The end of life

Days go by and I feel better. Francesca spends all the time she can by my side, and I believe she is the best medicine for both my body and my spirit. Things aren't easy for Francesca, juggling between work, children and volunteering at the hospital. She tells me that her ex-husband does everything to discredit her in the eyes of her children, and this is causing her much anxiety and sadness.

I'm in that state of half-sleep when the noises and the buzz in the corridors become more insistent, and I think I recognise Francesca's voice. Suddenly the sound of two explosions makes the glass and the wall tremble...
Francesca opens the door of my room and leans back on it, blood is trickling down from her mouth and she has her lifeless son in her arms, he has a big red stain on his chest. I scream *Noooo!!!* Horror and fear bursting out of me.
Francesca murmurs with a gasp: *Help me, my husband has shot my son...* I try to get out of bed, but my left leg won't hold me and I fall in a heap on the floor... I keep screaming until someone restrains me; with eyes veiled in tears I see one syringe, then another... while I sink into darkness, far away I hear another shot and then all sounds disappear.

There is an eerie silence in the hospital room, I have a strange taste in my mouth and a heavy head. I refuse to focus on what's happened and I look at the wall in front of the bed, without seeing it. A nurse comes in, then another, they check the monitor, change the drip bag and then, without saying a word, they leave.
The Professor enters, followed by the doctors who place the X-ray plates on the luminous glass of the wall and talk to each other, shake their heads, mumble a little more, and finally they leave.
Silence returns, I hope it was just a bad dream but deep inside I know it's not. When I open my eyes Katrin is there, next to the bed, I look into her eyes and let myself cry freely; with a faint voice I ask:
Francesca?
Arturo, we did everything we could, but she passed away half an hour after her son.
Why... WHY?

Her ex-husband couldn't accept the separation; he arrived at the hospital with their son to try to convince Francesca to return. When his son ran into his mother's arms rather than staying with him, he shot him. Francesca took her son in her arms and tried to hide in your room, but then he shot her in the back; after a few minutes a guard managed to kill him.

Every word pronounced by Katrin is a stab to my heart, but I know it's plainly the truth.

For now I've prescribed you some sedatives to get you through this... then it will take time... lots of time.

Fighting

There is a gloomy atmosphere of an antique metallic blue colour; the houses in the city are reduced to rubble. It looks like Berlin at the end of the war. People, mostly elderly or old before their time, move slowly with a sad, emaciated look, like puppets whose strings are being pulled by unfamiliar, clumsy beings. They are ancestral beings, who live in the dim light and that my eyes refuse to see; I know they are there, I know they are watching me. There is a little girl, she's young and of a delicate beauty, but she has a dead look about her, and this saddens and worries me. Far away, fading out, I hear Marlene Dietrich miming the tune of *Lili Marlene*, or maybe... I just imagine it. I am far away from this world.

The room is huge with a large window looking out to a black sea and an orange sky. A man enters wearing combat gear, his body is sturdy, his beard unkempt, his eyes and his appearance show great tiredness. There is no furniture in that room, the man props his weapon against the wall and sits on the floor with his back against the wall.

He's muttering: *Fight, still fight.*

Against the darker wall of the room there is another crouched shape I had not noticed before. It's woman of about thirty, her uniform makes her look very masculine, but there's still a hint of femininity. She, like the man in the other corner, has a sad, resigned look, she asks with a whisper: *How many of us are left?*

I don't know, the man replies, *maybe it's only you and me; from what I can see, this outpost is the only one left and will soon sink into blackness, like everything else.*

Why all this? The girl asks again. *I don't think there's a reason, we found ourselves in the wrong place, at the wrong time and that's all.* What the hell does that mean, why am I watching all this, how did I end up here... where... which dimension am I in?

I don't know where I am, I don't know how I moved, now I'm in a bed, maybe a clinic or a hospital, I cannot move, I'm immobilised, I can only wander with my eyes. There are other people around me, some people are standing, others speak, but I don't hear anything; I don't see anything clearly, besides the big window, perennially dark blue, on the other side maybe there is the sky... but it's not from this world... or at least the one wherea I think I live.

The tunnel

I hear a distant and unknown voice saying: *He's not improving, we have to try a different treatment.*
Someone else answers: *We can't do it here, we should send him to Egypt. There's a caravan leaving at the end of the week, going through the tunnel, he'll be in Cairo in five days.*
I'm totally confused: *Cairo, the tunnel, what the hell are they talking about?*
I feel that they are manhandling me and then moving me, my sight is confused and clouded, but I can feel the walls sliding, and after a while, I glimpse the entrance of a tunnel...
I feel movement and the continuous, hypnotic splashing of water.
I focus on this sound until I hear two people talking not too far away, even though I can't work out where they are.
The tunnel under the sea certainly was a great invention.
What it's made of, how can it withstand the pressure of thousands of tons of water?
I'm not a physicist, all I know is that it's an air tube with two different pressures: the internal one allows you to move normally, the outer one has a wall that works a bit like the Earth's atmosphere, separating the vacuum from space; however everything seems to be concentrated in an energy layer of a few microns.

The journey continues; my awareness is always blurred, and I wonder: *If this tunnel is so important and has existed for centuries, why has no one revealed it? Why have I never heard of it? Maybe it was kept secret for some obscure reason of power, or perhaps the price to pay is 'oblivion'.*

We continue the journey without knowing what the weather is like; in the distance I can see blurred images, sunken ships? traces of houses? of human artefacts? We also meet a caravan travelling in the opposite direction, and people on foot... I wonder: *Where have they come from? Where are they going?*

After a never-ending time, we go outside, it's evening, the sky is far away, and beyond the street lamps I can see the stars. The sweet warm air caresses my face. I've never been to Cairo, I have flown over it several times and once, while returning from Zimbabwe, as the flight was early, the pilot decided to descend en route so the passengers could see the pyramids from above.

Africa - many say that *if you know it, it will enter your heart and soul.* I think back to that journey where everything, like many of the events in my life, happened by chance.

In the footsteps of Livingstone

Harare Club

When we say Africa, some people think of that part of Africa that only exists in the more or less collective imagination, created by adventures, books and movies; I'm not entirely sure that what follows is a description of the true Africa: however, for me it's definitely what I thought I saw, perceived and I am trying to pass this on to you.

White and black

First impact at the Harare Club: *Excuse me sirs, you are not properly dressed.* I turn toward Walter and Valentina Incerpi, my travelling companions, and their look is as interrogative as mine. This Club is a real, perhaps last piece of Her Majesty's Kingdom, even if it's free and independent. We will have to change at least twice a day, for breakfast and for going out. Furthermore, if we want to spend a few minutes in the rooms intended for guests, well, that's three changes of clothes. But it's not bad, it's like catapulting back to the past; on the stairs with photos of past presidents, you breathe in the air of an aristocratic world that no longer exists. It is an exclusive world, complete with silverware, in the centre of Harare, in front of the Parliament building; except for some rare exceptions, the members are all white, and the attendants strictly black, exactly like the boy who wakes me up at six o'clock with coffee and the Herald, where I discover what I already knew: the percentage of HIV positivity is impressive and is growing out of all proportion.

Zimbabwe is not like South Africa, for better or worse, here black and white coexist, almost realising they are two faces of the same coin. The blacks, since 1980, have the political power, the whites the economic power; yet, society is changing, the shades are not so clear, and integration continues much better than in other parts of Africa. However, when I entered a supermarket in the centre, I felt like a white fly; the exact same feeling I once felt in a London tube train heading towards Balham. Even there I was the only white. What disturbed me most was realising that many of those I contacted were more embarrassed than me, for the simple fact that they were black.

In other words, if for some whites it may be easy to accept parity, for many of colour it is not the same.

Welcome to Victoria Falls

After a week visiting flower companies, we decided to have a few days' holiday. Sergio Pezzi, the expert in cold storage, returned to Italy; Stefano Cocchi, the consultant, stayed in town to persuade farmers to plant asparagus. We say farewell to the restaurant in Garibaldi Square (pure Tuscan), to the friends of '68, to the colonial-style old man at the 'Treasure Trove' and to the shadow man (A. Colin Shade); there's a direct plane to Victoria Falls and the beginning of our adventure. Three hours later we're at our hotel, a giant black man gives us the Welcome to Vic Falls!; a group is playing the local *marimba* music, we have fruit juice and then go to our rooms.

The style and the way of treating tourists isn't really so different from any hotel in the Caribbean, and it's hard to believe that you're in the Africa I mentioned before.

We booked the guide for our visit to one of the most beautiful waterfalls in the world, discovered in 1855 by the Scottish explorer David Livingstone; we arrive there after a quick look at the artisan village reconstructing and selling pieces of Africa.

The 'Smoke which Thunders' (*Mosi-oa-tunya*)

The waterfalls are more or less 150 million years old, the scientists calculate that then they were 150 kilometres further downstream; through the centuries they have moved backwards thanks to the constant erosion of the basaltic plateau on which the Zambezi river flows. Today they have a front of 1700 metres and are divided into five sectors: *Devil, Maine, Horseshoe, Rainbow* and *Eastern*. During the rainy season they have a flow rate of 545 million litres of water per minute, falling with a shocking noise, raising a cloud for over 500 metres. Hence the name 'Smoke which Thunders', given by the indigenous population (even older names are *Seongo* or *Thonguè* meaning the rainbow place). We book 'the Flight of Angels' for the next day over the 'Smoke Which Thunder's', and after a lot of negotiation with the blond girl at Avis, Walter also manages to get us free bicycles for the afternoon.

Zambia

We ride towards Zambia, you just have to cross the bridge, only 500 metres, over the Zambezi. The bikes have solid rubber tyres, if you don't pedal they don't move, even downhill.

At the checkpoint we have to pay 20 US dollars for our visas; Valentina is not yet 18, so this doesn't apply to her, then there's the customs declaration for the bicycles, as Zimbabwe considers them to be Zimbabwean property. So together with a truly mixed bag of humanity: from the South African with his camper, to the cross-border commuters who walk home, they don't have a passport like ours, but a legal paper – with countless stamps on it – we cross the bridge, we're in no-man's land, and then after a few metres a rather battered sign welcomes us to Zambia.

As real tourists, a photo is a must; I ask a black woman if she'd agree to pose with me, she says yes, but only shaking hands, which, with some surprise on her part, I do.

On the other side of the bridge there is poverty, you can see it with the naked eye, we are not yet at the level of the TV images, yet you can feel it in the air, it enters the skin and penetrates the soul.

We can't even understand why: they have waterfalls, the space to build hotels, to take advantage of the economic benefits of tourism like Zimbabwe, and yet... nothing; there is a lot of 'figuring it out' going on, to drink an orange juice you change currency on the black market, by selling some Zimba dollars at half the official value.

We return in the evening worn out, however the scenery was beautiful, and the effort was worthwhile.

After dinner with ad hoc music, at the casino – which is nothing but a bunch of old slot machines – I also win ten Zimba dollars (less than one euro) in pennies and I get envious looks from a whole lot of people!

On the other hand, the baboons crossing the streets towards the hotel are indifferent.

The 'Flight of Angels'

In the morning, on the plane for the 'Flight of Angels': the engine starts the old-fashioned way, with the attendant in front of the plane with the fire extinguisher ready; anyway we take off, the pilot is good, even if I feel like *Those Magnificent Men in Their Flying*

Machines, the ones, I mean, that were taking off with the ambulance behind – because this way, many more pilots could be saved. Once over the 'Smoke Which Thunders' I don't even think any more, I'm at one with my Nikon and I look at the world through the lens, one shot after another, the plunging water, the rainbow, the savannah.

Valentina, after a very tight turn, feels sick. In the Zambesi, hippos and elephants swim peacefully and don't care at all about that big mosquito up there, hovering in the air.

We land, we pay a visit to the giant baobab with the roar of the engines still in our ears and then we go downhill for a couple of kilometres, some of them really steep, to see the heroes of rafting on a rubber dinghy shooting the rapids for about fifty kilometres, including one woman who made half the descent on her bottom (I don't have to tell you what colour it was!). We don't have time for that experience, the plane for Kariba leaves in the afternoon.

Kariba

After a queue of almost an hour in the local bank, we can get some Zimba dollars and then souvenirs, here the ivory is sold per kilo, Zimbabwe has not signed the convention, but we opt for something not so bloody. The plane lands at Kariba, the dam built by the Italians, the bus that takes us to the hotel is packed with passengers, the enormous woman from UTC counts her flock several times, then checks the list and confirms that all the sheep are actually hers. We are at the Cutty Sark, right on the lake and here the scenery is less luxurious and definitely more safari. In the room it's clear that you're no longer connected to Europe, there are instructions for malaria, for buffaloes and for crocodiles (yes, the lake is full); it seems that every year about 150 people end up in the jaws of future shoes and handbags for women.

A nice dose of Autan (mosquito repellent), (I took the chloroquine on Tuesday), and I go out to enjoy the African sunset on Lake Kariba, it's beautiful! Perhaps it's here that exteriorisation begins. At some times, it's not necessary, in others it is, because you look *out*, however, we talk less. In the evening I write to Ezio, my friend who's in hospital in Genoa, and I seem to be really far away.

In the early morning Valentina discovers a couple of buffaloes still asleep a few metres from our rooms, maybe... maybe... we are approaching Africa. Here too, just like the outskirts of Harare, there's a huge movement of people from unpredictable paths and disappearing into others, it seems that they appear out of nowhere and disappear into nothingness. We linger on the beach and round about, we buy some embroidered tablecloths to please the sellers and we wait for the next plane for Mana Pools.

Mana Pools

After a couple of hours waiting at the airport and meeting a French woman who warns us about the buffaloes (an American and his guide had just been killed by one — indifferent to the nationality or status of their prey), our pilot comes forward, blond, moustached, knees full of scars (he was a motocross fan). He bluntly infers to strap ourselves in well in the little Navaho, there is turbulence up there, but we consider ourselves veterans.

I'm sitting next to the pilot, Walter and Valentina behind. The plane moves slowly, the tower gives the OK, and we're away. I start to worry when I see that the blond man holding the trim with his knee; while crossing the mountains the plane thrown about, I focus on my breathing and try to control my nausea; Valentina does not make it, and clings to her father, but it's not only the nausea, it's fear and she says: *Dad, I'm shitting myself.*

Slowly, between one jolt and another we make it to the other side, and the flight becomes calmer. We are in sight of the landing strip: red clay in the middle of the bush (the savannah), we're there but the plane's engine has stopped working, we touch ground by the skin of our teeth! A Land Rover is approaching, driven by a boy about 20 years old, dark sunglasses, anorak, looking like a character in a Wilbur Smith novel.

There are also four Americans, one is a lawyer from Arizona; they apologise because while waiting they drank our beer (the excellent low-alcohol Zambesi). The pilot with everything he has, just a screwdriver, starts to disassemble the plane. With Rob (the guide) we go by Jeep to look for a tool box at the Mana Pools camp, for nothing. Kariba is alerted by radio, Rob tells us that we have to wait, he can't leave the pilot and the Americans alone with the wild beasts nearby, and so we spend one hour after another in the shade of thin bushes.

After four hours another Land Rover, from the Ruchomeci Camp, comes to see what's happened.

Rob stays there, after a couple of hours the spare plane arrives; ours will be repaired by the mechanics who arrive by land the next day.

The frontiers of adventure

After another hour and a half on the jeep we arrive at the camp; Leslie (the only woman and the manager, even if the male members didn't agree with this definition) is there, waiting for us with our lunch, even if it's already 6.00 p.m., we're hungry, and eat without knowing that an hour later we're also going to have dinner.

She gives us each a bungalow, thatched roof, a 50 cm wall and wire mesh with curtains at the glassless windows.

We have hot water and light provided by generators just for a couple of hours a day.

Leslie asks us to sign a form to exempt Shearwater (the company that manages Ruckomeci Camp) from any responsibility.

After dinner we get to know the other six guides: except for John and Basil, they are all young, and are there to earn some money before going to University. It also turns out that the camp is open six months a year, that it accepts no more than 15 guests at a time, and that you have to book at least six months in advance.

After sunset, a beer in the outdoor bar, a chat and bed at 9 p.m. At about 11 p.m. all hell breaks loose: grunts, sounds, screams, the noise of broken branches, metal pots beaten, I try to look out, it's pitch black and I see nothing, all I can do is just go back to bed and try to sleep.

The next morning it turns out that the camp had been visited not only by the hippos, but also by Joseph, a big elephant that, while feeding on branches and grass, managed to demolish the kitchens. It will take three days for the attendants to rebuild the whole thing. The morning is beautiful, despite the cold; Basil takes us by jeep to see the savannah, to look for the animals. We see everything, except giraffes, they don't live in this part of Zimbabwe, and the lions, who are hidden. Valentina comes looking for me, she has lost her father. Walter, a real fan of hunting (only photographic this time), has left the camp without a guide, and this is forbidden.

I go after him and find him following the river; we see the skeleton of a hippo, a crocodile plunging into the water, and hippos on a small island in the Zambesi; after a while I warn him that his daughter is tired of being a dad-sitter. We go back to the sun-scorched camp, happy with our escapade. In the afternoon we go canoeing with Derek. Valentina is reluctant, but she follows us anyway (and she enjoys it).

We gently descend the Zambezi, in silence; Derek has a gun, he hardly speaks, we are doing the same, we just enjoy the beauty of the water and the animals in the wild. After a while we stop at a clearing along the shore to rest.

I sit and look around, I start to feel the vibrations of the earth, water and air, I perceive the life forms in the vicinity, the snakes and scorpions that are beginning to awaken over there, the animals and the rustlings that have a meaning. All of a sudden I find myself at one with this land and I understand it, there is also violence, not rough, not stupid, not without reason, like man's, but natural and in its way perhaps not useless.

Walter calls me, we go back to the camp, that night I sleep peacefully, I am familiar with the sounds that surround me, but am woken up by the park guards shooting, they have to reduce the number of elephants by 1,000 (in Zimbabwe there are 10,000) and impala by 5,000.

In the morning the guides are nervous, Basil and John are worried: *Is it possible they don't understand, it's true that the drought makes it difficult, that there're too many animals , but don't they understand that tourists pay thousands of dollars to see them and they are killing them.*

Blood on the track
Ruchomeci Camp isn't large, 50 sq. km in the Mana Pools Natural Park, on the border with Zambia. Here hunting is absolutely forbidden, the guards shoot at anyone carrying weapons, although many poachers from Zambia cross the Zambezi in a canoe in search of

ivory. In fact, all the rhinoceroses (which are in danger of extinction, there are only 70 in the whole of Zimbabwe) have their horns surgically removed; the problem is that the poachers don't know this. Later, in Harare we discover that two or three poachers were killed by the guards, just a stone's throw away from us. The traces of night hunting can be seen, there is blood on the trail.

At the camp there are only the three of us, an English couple from Nottingham, birdwatchers (there are more than 5,000 species in Zimbabwe), and a woman from Zurich. We walk in the savannah, John armed with a rifle, but we hardly see anything. In the afternoon, five Catalan girls arrive, with my very South American Spanish, I discover that they're waiting for canoes to descend the Zambezi up to Mozambique, a nice trip! They also have to sign the exemption form and look at me terrified; they've had to pay a lot of money to run who knows what risks!

Looking for lions

In fact, the danger isn't so great, but the fact is that they have never been in a canoe, and this is more than obvious when, half an hour later, the current pulls them away sideways. Valentina and Walter choose the canoe too. I ask if I can follow Basil to see where the lions have gone.

With the jeep we cross the entire reserve, we penetrate into the most hidden ravines, we find their tracks and follow them like bloodhounds until late: but we're unlucky, the lions (all 12 of them) and all the other animals are too scared, they are well hidden. But this research has its charm, apparently Basil is unarmed, or at least he wants me to think so; but actually, he carries a bag that he never lets go of. He is burned by the sun, he hardly speaks, he is over sixty, and he really worries about his animals. We stop in a prairie nicknamed adrenaline field, as you can find anything from elephants to buffalo to lions within it. With a beer in our hands we watch the sunset. I ask him if he ever goes to the capital, he replies that he has no reason, he spent his youth as a soldier, he fought in Mozambique; he's divorced, his ex-wife and two children live in South Africa, two more sons in Harare, he lives here.

Now it's my turn to answer his questions and I don't have much to say; even if I'm European, my life isn't so very different. In the end, we discover that we're not different at all.

Slowly we return to the camp, and in the dark, with the cold air cutting my face, I think that maybe I have found an old lion.

We remain one more day and a night, we say goodbye to our friends in the Ruchomeci Camp and then, together with the English couple, we go with Rob to the airport.

The plane this time is an old Cessna, it taxis out on the clay track raising a light red cloud of powdery dust but the pilot is still the same. Crossing the mountains towards Kariba is even more painful than before, but when we get there, the north end of the bush is burning. We realise we've been lucky, we've seen a completely wild island that in ten years' time will no longer exist.

We have to spend a few more days in Harare and after visiting the floriculturists, one evening we go and pay a visit to Pino, a Sicilian with an Alfa Romeo Duetto and a restaurant. I eat just a little, for three hours I have a fever; I would like to switch to Lariam, but Pino is friendly and it's nice to hear the story of his life in Africa.

Anthony Fischer

It's our last visit, tomorrow our plane leaves for Athens via Larnaca. I have already mentioned the company and Fischer, but not anything about his house: it's simply beautiful, with a thatched roof and very tastefully furnished. One look at his books and his CDs: all classical music, from the '*greats*', and Angelo Lamberti, the CEO of Idrotermserre, immediately springs to mind. He loves music, theatre and life; I think that Anthony, besides being a leader, is also a great philosopher.

Outside, a huge bougainvillea is in bloom, and, on the other side, a weirdo lying on the grass with a book in his hand. A Benedictine father tells me the story of the Fischer family; they have been in Zimbabwe for over 100 years, and he tells me that it was thanks to Anthony that a Benedictine community was founded here. The weirdo has a pigtail and is moving in a strange way, he asks me questions that at first seem stupid and meaningless; but after I think about them for a moment I discover that actually there's a logic to them, the questions are deep and sharp-edged, and I begin to think that he is taking the Mickey. A battle of words begins, he's extraordinarily intelligent, I need total concentration and I struggle to keep up with him.

Later, I find out that he's one of the most renowned economists in Zimbabwe who pretends to be poor and stupid just to avoid paying taxes.

Anthony gives us as a preview of a new flower, he's friendly, he serves lunch himself and explains everything simply.

Back to the past.

An unpublished poem by Edward N. Bent comes to mind:

What's it worth, one elephant or gazelle
To our city lives and cars and stress?
More and more, we have become much less;
A bullet lying next to the ornament.

Faith

We travel through the Cairo streets towards the suburbs, I observe the palms, the bougainvillea and the shape of the houses, square, modular, low, similar to those of Israeli villages.

We are in the eastern part of the city, in a quiet neighbourhood, away from the bustle of the centre. We enter a house with a large hall, there are many other people, mostly lying down in an orderly fashion, as if in a queue; others are moving about.

Distant voices: *We can only wait and hope it rains. If it rains, the water will rise from the floor,* and I think: *If I get wet, I'll feel better, What kind of cure is this, what does it mean?* I have no answers, I tell myself that all in all, faith does not need explanations... but do I have faith?

The days pass, nothing happens, it's sunny, and the sky is clear.

Excited voices speak of our return.

I'm not aware that we have travelled, but I find myself back in Bergamo.

And I'm unaware of subsequent journeys or of being in that same room for days on end. Still, motionless... it's necessary to have patience and... faith.

I make the last part of the trip back from Cairo by ship. An old ship, huge, with ageing paintwork, the traces of innumerable coats of paint applied to battle against the salt water clearly visible.

I'm still motionless, somewhere in a fairly spacious cabin. I hear different noises, sometimes clear, sometimes muffled. At some point the noises become more consistent. We aren't moving, I hear talk of something in the boiler room having broken down, the engines are no longer working... we are at the mercy of the sea and the wind, I think: *Like my life without Francesca.*

We dock in the port of Salerno with the usual movement and bustle accompanying a ship's arrival. Not far from the port there is Sant'Antonio di Pontecagnano, where Lucio and Maria live... the Amalfi Coast, Ravello, the buffalo mozzarella; I would like to visit it with Francesca... I would like to stop for a moment.

I'm in a strange room, I don't know if it's a hospital or a dormitory.

The lights are dim, people move about slowly, as in slow motion, and there's never any sunlight coming through the windows. They talk to me about spaces and dimensions that are far beyond my reach and my level of understanding. I no longer have any secure points of reference, I'm travelling through an absurd and unknown situation, all its elements are moving in a way that seems to me to be totally illogical.

Where is Francesca? In whichever universe she is, in whichever dimension she has ended up, no matter how far away she is, I have to look for her.

The journey continues, this time we change direction, from the north I go down to central Italy; Adelio Gaviraghi told me he has a production unit in the Marche, I don't know where it is, but with a bit of luck I'll find it. I walk and walk down roads and paths, plants on their edges, bushes and agaves, certainly *Agave americana* and its variegated form, but a little bit further there is also a fine specimen of *Agave attenuata*.

My journey continues. I arrive in Sicily. My first stop is Giarre, birthplace of the legendary Dr Carlo Calì and of the Silver Carnation prize.

The first time I was in Giarre was September 1990, when the Cultural Association I fiori di Giarre e dell'Etna, chaired by Dr. Calì, awarded me the Silver Carnation prize. Since then I have collaborated with Doctor Calì on all the following editions.

Doctor Calì is dressed in a cream-coloured linen suit and a white Panama hat. On this occasion, I have the impression that Giarre has assumed the look of New Orleans. Calì makes me a request that seems crazy, he wants me to write a message and fax it to North Korea.

I remind him that because of his business affairs in North Korea, my acquaintance Yang Bin of Asia Agribusiness was jailed in China and is serving 20 years in prison. Calì insists and tells me that his fax will not cause problems. I shake my head and I quickly go away. Now I don't know where I am, certainly not in a city, everything is silent and there are very few people on the streets. I arrive at a house at sunset, it's oddly built, definitely not a farm. Maybe it's a monastery... a man is there waiting for me. I can't say whether he's a monk or a friar even though he's wearing a brown habit. He asks me to trust him and follow him. He explains that in order to escape my situation I must have faith. I can't fully understand who or what it is I should have faith in, and my being simply wanders into an infinite space and my awareness fades away.

I'm stuck, motionless, maybe in a church or a building that looks like one; there are some strange lights — are they coming from different-sized candles?. Even the smells are special, I think I recognise the scent of incense mixed with a faint smoke smell.

I know that the sun is out there, that there are people, I think I might be near Pione... there is the Chapel, the *Locanda dei Due - The Inn of the Two*. Is it possible everything has changed so much? I used to come here as a child, together with my father and mother, we had a chestnut wood and a small piece of land at the *Serri* (the wood of *Quercus cerris*). Not far away, following the path in the woods, there is a spring, they say it is holy. One day, here, Francesca and I made love, simply, on the ground, and then, with such sweetness, we came out of the woods holding hands. It was hot and Francesca, to provoke me further, had not worn any knickers. We visited Bardi Castle and there, hidden in a dark corner of a room in the basement, standing, we made love again, passionately, furiously, soothing that desire to become one.

I'm lying on what looks like an altar, it's hard, I can't move. My eyes wander towards the light in the windows and the doors and I think: *Is it possible that religion has such powerful symbols?; Is it possible I can't overcome my thoughts about these symbols blocking me and preventing me from getting up and leaving?.*

Is anyone making suggestions? I don't know... all I can think is: *I can't run away, I can't pretend it doesn't exist, I can't go around it... I have to go through it... I have to understand what it is... this is the only way I can be free.*

The only one you owe faith to and trust is yourself... Everything else is not only impossible but it is the sign of a false messiah...

Where had I read that? Almost certainly in *Illusions: The Adventures of a Reluctant Messiah* by Richard Bach. Is faith really the last bastion of awareness? Can you really not go beyond being? Should I therefore believe that I can do it? Does action depend on and derive from faith or can it exist independently? And love, what is love? Do I love myself deeply? Is this why I feel I love Francesca the same as I love myself? But... does love have boundaries? Limits?

I am desperately looking for answers, I'm lost somewhere, and I miss Francesca terribly, I miss her gaze, her smile, without her I'm unable to move, lost in silence and nothing and nobody has the power to shake me from this space-time immobility.

How can I change the thoughts immobilising me in this numbness?

Maybe it was faith that pushed me to go to Israel for the first time in 1986; I thought then that the reason for my trip was floriculture and, if someone had told me otherwise, I would have considered them crazy. Then, one day, the third or the fourth time I visited Israel, Ester Arditti, my guide, told me something I still think about today.

Ester Arditti Bornstein

The Consorzio dei Florovivaisti Comaschi are organising a study trip to Israel, I decide to go, it will certainly be interesting for my magazine and in any case that country and its history have always fascinated me. One evening, a few days before departure, I contact Franco Cereda, flower importer and wholesaler. He, together with Max Weijel, were responsible for setting up Israeli floriculture.

Franco, tired of the fluctuating prices of gladioli, took a bag of bulbs with him on one trip and, in the Negev desert, showed Weijel how they had to be planted. The first cut gladioli flowers were exported by Danziger and Franco was the first customer. He still remembers: *The flowers were beautiful, even if the stems were not very long and the label 'Grown in Israel by Danziger' was almost bigger than the flowers!*

I had known this company since I had attended the school at Minoprio, where I read an article by Michael Danziger about *Gypsophila* in the 'Florist's Review'. In fact, the company Dan Danziger Flower Farm owes much of its fortune to this plant. Franco gave me the telephone number of a friend of his, someone called Giora Wallis, from the plant department of Agrexco (the public-private company that at that time oversaw exports) and told me to contact him just in case.

From Linate we fly to Rome and, after the customary checks and questions by Israeli security, we fly to Tel-Aviv with El-Al company We land to the notes of 'Welcome to Israel'.

Two Italian speaking guides, Ester Arditti and Aliza Cohen, are waiting to accompany us to our hotel in Jerusalem. It is now evening and our neighbourhood is on the opposite side to the Arab one, which is more famous and picturesque. Together with a small group of other guests I wander through the nearby streets, but at night, in this part of the city, it is empty and soon we return to the Hotel. Aliza, our Israeli guide, advises us not to go to the old city — in her opinion, the Arabs are dangerous — but none of us wants to venture into an unknown part of the Holy City. Ester was born in Bulgaria and at the beginning of World War II was a refugee with her family in Livorno. Aged eleven, she had run away from home and tried to emigrate to Israel; she finally did so with her brother when she was sixteen. Despite her young age she joined the army and trained to become a nurse. On the night of 29 November 1955, she was on duty, it was cold and raining, a Mosquito plane was struck by lightning and fell. Ester rescued the navigator and although the ammunition was exploding, she returned to the plane to rescue the pilot too, just before the plane burst into flames. For this act she earned the *Zion Leshevac* medal, pinned on to her chest by General Moshe Dayan himself. After a period of leave Ester continued her work as a nurse and was the first Israeli woman to drive an ambulance. During the 'Six-Day War' (5-10 June 1967) she joined the parachutists who entered the city of Jerusalem under enemy fire; Ester rescued the wounded soldiers and for this reason she was called *the angel of the parachutists*.

She did the same during the 'Yom Kippur' war. In 1973 she was awarded the *Itur Amofet*. Later she chose to become a tourist guide, which allowed her to best express her love for the land of Israel.

Two or three of us meet up in the room of our Italian guide, Eleonora, she has accompanied us throughout the trip. She's a mature woman from Seveso, certainly not a beauty but brilliant. Eleonora says she has read books by a certain Carlos Castaneda which *made her flip;* she can't clearly say what these books contain, but she strongly recommends us to read them. When I returned to Italy I bought *The teachings of Don Juan* and, in the following years, all his other books. Castaneda is certainly a controversial figure, but the teachings of Don Juan Matus, which he narrates, certainly make us look at the world from another point of view. Maybe I don't have enough faith, I have so many questions that have been with man since man existed. Studying philosophy has left me with a very open mind, but has also led me to consider that functional truths exist and that absolutes are not achievable.

Maybe our human condition also prevents us from having a vision of the totality, the same as in the *Zen Ry'an-ji* garden in Kyoto, where it is impossible to see all 15 rocks which are arranged in groups of five, two,three, two, three, regardless of where you stand. This perhaps symbolises the limits of human nature.

I don't believe in any guru or messiah; even if I was brought up as a Catholic, I have a lot of doubts.

Since I believe the problem is unsolvable, at least from a human point of view, I have left everything open since I visited Arenzano. My mother was very religious and one of her dreams was to visit the *Santuario del Bambin Gesù*. So, one day, I took my mother, her sister Lina and my aunt Claudia to Arenzano (Genoa). I had never been there, even though I had passed through hundreds of times, on the motorway, when travelling to Sanremo, France and Spain.

While the three godly women were praying, I waited for them, sitting on a bench at the back of the Church, a little bored, so I had plenty of time to reflect. I was fantasising, and I asked myself: *Let's assume that God exists and that I can speak to him and that he can answer me. What would I ask him? Of course, I would rather ask him for something, not for myself but for the people I love. So what could I ask him for? That they be healthy, happy…*

That's when I realised that I could wish that the people I love were healthy and happy, but not force them to be so, it would be a terrible violation of their freedom and it would limit them.

So, going back to my hypothetical creation, mentally I told him: *It's okay, I understand, leave things as they are, whether you're there or not, that does not stop me from trying to follow an ethical and moral path making me at ease with my conscience.*

The Consortium had organised the trip with a travel agency that only planned visits to the holy places and the Bahai Gardens in Haifa. For the visit, the group of Italians is divided in two, a group with Ester and the other with Aliza. I decide to go with Ester: Aliza was against the Arabs and I believe that my choice was a good one. Ester is Jewish, but all the Arabs know her and respect her, and she greets everyone in a friendly way. As we enter the Arab side of Jerusalem from the Gate of Excrement (Dung Gate), accessing the western wall, the one we call the Wailing Wall, she explains the cornerstones of the Jewish religion and the rules for visiting the Arab side without causing any incident. Tourists are well liked by the Arabs because they represent a vital economic resource, the only rule that must be respected is not bothering their women; Ester tells us that even looking directly into the eyes of an Arab woman can be seen as an offence... *The eyes are the door of the soul.*

We immerse ourselves in the tide of people, colours, perfumes, smells, and sounds, all mixed with ancestral memories and thoughts of love and hope. There is a lot of humanity in this place; you feel its history penetrating deep and I feel some way towards belonging to this world... it is the first time I see it, but I get the feeling I have known it forever. I am the last in the queue with Vittorio, and we stop to marvel at a shop with a large collection of spices; when we leave our group has disappeared, swallowed up by the great human tide coming and going.

We don't lose heart, we know that we have to meet back at the bus at eleven, and we quietly continue the visit on our own. At eleven, we go back to the point of entry at the Dung Gate: there are many buses, but ours is not there. Back then, there were no mobile phones and we didn't know how to contact the rest of the group. At half past eleven, we finally see our bus arrive: neither of us had understood that the meeting was on the opposite side, at the Damascus Gate. The guides, who judiciously count their sheep, realised that two were missing and so came back to look for us.

In the afternoon, we visit the Bahai gardens in Haifa, yet there is increasing dissatisfaction as there is no professional visit scheduled. In the evening, when I return to the hotel, I phone Giora Wallis and, in my best possible English, I tell him that Franco Cereda had suggested I contact him to organise a visit or two to some companies. Giora replies that he's available, but it would be better, to save time, if I went to Lod by my own means. I meet Vittorio and I tell him that I have a meeting at Agrexco in the morning, at the Ben Gurion airport in Tel Aviv, and that I will go there by taxi: if he wants to join me, we can divide the expenses and he is welcome.

I inform the guides, and at 8 a.m. a taxi takes us to Tel Aviv. Giora is friendly, looks after us and takes us on a visit to different companies; at noon we eat for free in the Granot Kibbutz.

I also meet Itzik Gernstein, who on subsequent visits, together with Giora, Michael Eisinger, Eliah Spiegel, Michael and Gaby Danziger will become great friends. We return happy that evening and return to Tel Aviv the following day. Among the companies we visited were

BenZur, Danziger, Getzler, David Kaholi, Cohen, Peled, Solomon, Kibbutz Yagur, Mashiach, Aviv Packinghouse, Histhil, Hochman Schor. We explain to Giora that there is another group of floriculturists with us in Jerusalem and they are limited to seeing only tourist places, so he decides to talk to the travel agency and with the guides. The next day – by bus – everyone gets to see at least four iconic companies.

In the following years I returned to Israel several times and I was well known by all the Israeli nursery companies and institutions, and I no longer needed guides to move around.

From 28-30 June 1993 an international floriculture conference was to be held at the Carlton Hotel in Tel Aviv. The participation fee is quite high, considering that I also have to pay for the trip and the hotel. Yet, I decide to participate nonetheless: one of the speakers there is Robert Zurel, the largest exporter of flowers and plants in the world. I contact several friends to see if any of them want to come to Israel with me. Three of them decide to accompany me, Luigi Cereda, Paolo Zacchera and Andrea Orlandelli. Having arrived in Tel Aviv, as the membership fee included just one companion, Andrea and I participate in the conference, while Luigi and Paolo visit the south of Israel on their own with a rental car. In Israel the Sabbath is a holiday and we will use the day to visit Jerusalem together. On Friday afternoon I reflect on our visit to the holy city for the next day, and I conclude that I don't know enough about Jerusalem to guide my friends. Ester comes immediately to mind, but I don't have her phone number and the only thing I know is that she lives in Jerusalem.

I ask the hotel porter if he can help me, and I explain that Ester Arditti is the only woman honoured twice in Israel.

The concierge has heard of her, but is also puzzled, Arditti is her maiden name and the phone will be registered in her husband's name.

Ten minutes later he hands me a piece of paper with the inscription: Ester Arditti Bornstein and the phone number, smiling, telling me: *It was easy, Ester is too famous and well-known.*

I phone Ester somewhat embarrassed, it's Friday night and I have to ask her for help the next day. *Ester, you don't remember me, but I remember you very well, you were my first guide in Israel in 1986; are you free tomorrow to be our guide in Jerusalem?*

The next day we meet in a large building on Herzel Avenue, at the entrance to the city. We arrive a few minutes before the scheduled time, I know that Ester lives nearby, and after a few minutes we see her arrive on foot. Petite, with a hat and glasses, she has not changed. She approaches and says in Italian: *Good morning, which of you is Arturo?* Once she has identified me she says smiling: *You were clever,* so I ask her: *Why Ester?* And she, *Bless you, boy, how could I say no to someone who tells me: you were my first guide and I remember you...!*

We visit Jerusalem and this time, being only the four of us, Ester's explanations are much more in-depth, and we have plenty of time even to see corners of the old city not normally visited by groups. In the Basilica of the Holy Sepulchre, my companions visit what is believed to be the place where Jesus was crucified.

Ester and I wait for them outside in the shade.

At some point she says to me: *You know I got into Jerusalem with the parachutists and here there was nothing, everything had been devastated. Everything you see now was fabricated by priests later; the same happened in Bethlehem and in many other places. Regardless of what you see now, you keep on returning to this land, why? What is it calling you here every time? Evidently beyond what you see, maybe something is really there.* All I can say is: *I don't know Ester, floriculture is my job and here I have something new to write about; however, the truth is that I am attracted by these places and I don't know why.*

We never talked about it again, not even a couple of years later, when I organised a visit for the members of the Flormercati Cooperative.

We continued the visit of the city and we stopped for lunch at Ester's butcher friend who had a small restaurant on one of the many streets of ancient Jerusalem. Despite the scorching sun, the restaurant, with its marble walls, was cool. The kitchen was across the street and we had the most delicious lamb ribs.

In the afternoon we visited Bethlehem, passing the checkpoint with Ester was really easy. All the military knew her, likewise the Arabs on the other side. In Bethlehem, Ester urges us to buy something from the Palestinians: *This way, you help peace...*

When we brought her back to Beit Hakerem and before leaving her, I asked how much we owed her. Ester answers: *'Nothing'.*
How nothing, Ester, you gave up your free day for us?
If you really want to give me something, please take out a subscription to Topolino (the Italian Mickey Mouse) for my children.
When I returned to Italy, I took out the subscription and we divided the amount. In the following years I continued to renew it, until she told me: *Please stop, my children have grown up now...*

The last time I saw her, Ester proudly showed me her certified tourist license issued by the Jordanian State. Once the border with Jordan opened, she accompanied tourists to Petra (the Colourful City), considered one of the 'Seven Wonders of the World'. I promised myself to go there with her, but I never did manage it. Ester died of cancer in February 2003, I learned this from Aliza Cohen, who I bumped in to accidentally during one of my last trips to Israel. Much later I found out that she's buried in Livorno (Leghorn). Ester asked to be buried with her family there. I asked my friend Furio to find out where her tomb is, I want to go and say thank you to her one last time.
The great little Ester has conquered a place in the history of Israel and a belvedere (view point) on the bank of the river Jordan, near the Roman Bridge which connects Israel to Jordan, has been dedicated to her memory.

I have always had faith in myself, even in my most difficult moments I used to say: *I can do it.* Most often everything has happened by chance, without planning anything. It was enough for me to be calm and to look to the future without fear, with the curious eyes of a child. All my life has been a succession of random occurrences, always lucky ones. Like that time in Denmark.

Anna Jole and Bodil

It's a hot and unpleasant day; Aldo is working in the other room, I smoke my umpteenth cigarette... today I've lost count... blue swirls of smoke waft out of the window. My eyes are on the video, but my mind is blank, I know that something is about to happen and not just because my inner voice tells me, I know, I have just to wait.

The telephone rings: *Good morning, Dr. Croci, I am Einar Olav Nilssen, I wanted to invite you to the open day at Dahenfeldt in Denmark... I would be very pleased...*

I immediately say yes... I had visited Odense and the Dahenfeldt a few years before for the *CEJH* (*Communauté Européenne de Jeunes de l'Horticulture*) Congress and I knew this company to be one of the most important in the world for the hybridisation of begonias: this could provide an interesting article for my magazine. A few days later I receive another phone call from Nilssen: *I'm embarrassed to ask you a great favour... Scandinavian Airlines charge for only one single ticket if a husband and wife are travelling together. Do you mind if I say that you are the husband of my employee, Dr. Anna Jole Tonelli? ...You know, it would save me a lot of money.* I don't know the girl, however I answer: *No problem.* On the day of departure, I arrive at Linate airport and head to the SAS check in; there is Dr. Nilssen, Piero Marino, Nives Silotto and a girl I don't know; I approach and ask, smiling: *Where is my wife?* Anna Jole has a simple, natural and captivating smile. After the introductions we head for the boarding area. The flight to Copenhagen passes without incident; from there we have a connection to Odense.

The first time I visited that city was in 1978, for the Young European Congress at Søhus Gartneriskole. My first contact with that association was in 1970. I didn't know it then, but that meeting many years ago had a positive influence on my life.

Odense for me represented the city of Hans Christian Andersen and of Kristen, whom I met at the congress. Kristen was a brilliant and beautiful woman, in those days everyone tried to flirt with her, but smart woman that she was, knew how to defend herself very well. Obviously, I was attracted to her too; as her husband said: *Maybe because you Italians are dark haired, and she's blonde.* Kristen, who

I got to know better in Annecy, had given me a copy of the *Little Prince* in French.

We arrive in Odense and everything runs according to plan; Jens Tøfte is waiting for us and accompanies us on a visit to the Dahenfeld field trial, in the evening dinner in a typical restaurant and finally bed.

The day after we split up, Einar and Cristina go to Aarhus for a business meeting, Piero and Nives have private tours. Anna Jole and I, accompanied by Edy, a Jiffy agent on the island of Funen, will visit some flower companies. After two visits, I look at the clock and it is nearly midday; since it is Sunday I suggest that Edy accompany us to the airport, so that then he can have lunch with his family. The plane to Copenhagen leaves at two o'clock, we check in and with our boarding cards in our hands we say goodbye to Edy.

We have a couple of hours to relax at the airport bar. We sit at a table and everyone is lost in their own thoughts. With Anna Jole, I'm not yet confident enough to go beyond friendly formality.

I look around, the bar is almost empty, but a little further on there is a table occupied by a blonde woman who's watching me; I glance at her, then look a little more deliberately until our eyes meet. She timidly starts smiling and so do I. I look away for a moment and say in an indifferent tone to Anna Jole: *Look at that lady... it's in the bag!* Anna Jole replies as any woman would have done: *Men, you are all the bloody same.* I don't really care about her answer, in fact, a minute later all three of us are sitting at the same table chatting quietly in English.

The woman is called Bodil and she's going to Copenhagen to meet her husband, she's enthusiastic about Italy and she's very interested in Etruscan art; her husband deals with antiquities or something like that.

Suddenly there is an loudspeaker announcement, due to the fog our plane will not be able to leave, the airport management informs us that a bus will take us to a small airport in the north where there is hopefully no fog.

At this point, Bodil states: *They will have to organise the bus, then it will take at least one hour to get there, then another hour to organise*

the flight: you will surely miss the connection for Milan with the 5 o'clock flight. If we run quickly to the station and take a train, we can get to Copenhagen for 4.00 p.m., with a quick taxi you could do it...
We decide in a second, we leave the airport and make for the carpark. Bodil's car is a Russian Lada that has known better times, half rusty, smooth tyres, the window deflectors have not been opened for a long time.

Anna Jole sits behind me, I am next to Bodil, who never stops talking. She drives erratically, she doesn't take any notice of the traffic lights, She wanders all over the lane, often crossing part of the opposite one, and... she is speeding. I pretend nothing is happening, and I calmly and coolly answer her questions; who knows what Anna Jole is thinking, I turn a couple of times and she is looking at me with a poker face.

We enter the car park at Odense station at high speed, there is not a single parking place available. Bodil does not hesitate to use the parking places reserved for the post office saying: *I worked for twenty years at the post office, I should have some rights.*
I reflect, thinking that yes, maybe the car could be left there for a little while, but not for a couple of days, it's excessive; they wouldn't steal that old Lada, but she could get a fine. It's not my business, anyway, and she should know what she's doing.

We enter the station and Bodil, with the speed of summer lightening, goes to the only ticket counter; and starts to argue with the employee, everything becomes more and more intense and confused; I don't understand anything in Danish, but I have the feeling that something is wrong... Bodil is waving her hands, getting more and more excited, and she points us out to the employee.
I look at Anna Jole to see if maybe she has understood something, but from her face, clearly not. I approach the counter; Bodil already has her ticket in her hand. Addressing the clerk, I ask: *Two single tickets to Copenhagen*, and she answers: *Oh! Two single tickets,* she looks relieved and gives me the tickets showing me the price.
I pay, and mentally I wonder what on earth the argument was all about; I give up asking for explanations.
As if nothing has happened, Bodil suggests with a hopeful smile:

There's 20 minutes before the train leaves, we have plenty of time to have a beer at the bar.

The barmaid is a typical Danish girl, stout but pleasant, along with the beers she brings me the bill; I pay, and she gives me my change. A few minutes later, Bodil calls the barmaid and in Danish starts to argue heatedly; the two women are really angry, at a certain point the furious barmaid takes out a couple of crowns from her wallet, puts them on the table, upset, and walks away.

I ask Bodil what is happening, and she says that I had not been given my change. I call the barmaid over and return the coins saying: *I'm sorry, you already gave me my change*, she takes the coins and moves away, glaring angrily at Bodil.

The train for Nyborg arrives, from there we have to take the ferry and get back on the train on the other side, destination Copenhagen. Bodil advances down the corridor looking for the smoking area, Anna Jole and I meekly follow her.

Finally, we find a compartment with only two people inside. We go in and find ourselves in a foul-smelling environment, full of stale air and smoke. I sit in front of Bodil, Anna Jole next to me, is clearly uneasy. That environment is bothering me, a heavy smoker; I can imagine how it is for her, a non-smoker. Bodil lights a cigarette, I do the same, but I extinguish it almost immediately. The only other time I was ashamed to smoke was at Bangkok airport: the smoking area was a crystal room with vacuum cleaners, but it took only a minute for your clothes to be impregnated with the sour smell of tobacco. The ticket collector passes through, punches our tickets and smiles at us with a look of compassion.

We chat about this and that, until the train stops. After a few minutes Bodil suddenly jumps up, grabs her bag and screams: *We have to get off!* We head for the door. Bodil gets out first, Anna Jole follows her and... the guard is whistling for the train's departure and the doors are closing; Anna Jole has one foot on the lowest step and one on the ground, exactly in the middle of the doors that are closing.

I am yanking on one side, Bodil on the other. Anna Jole doesn't even have time to scream. Luckily the guard realises what's happening, blocks the train and hurries over to us: *This is not your station, get back on the train immediately, and don't get off until I will tell you.*

We go back and sit down, no one says a word, all the way to Nyborg, near the ferryboat.

I follow Bodil down the stairs, but this time a little more suspicious, Anna Jole remains impassive.

Once on board Bodil says: *Let's go and have a drink, I'll pay.* The bar is almost deserted. *Do you know the Gammel Dansk bitters? Noo?!?!... You must try it.* I reply: *Bodil, we've eaten hardly anything, it's better not to drink strong alcohol on an empty stomach.* A moment later we are holding a little bottle of *Gammel Dansk* each. I think to myself that it's a bit like our *amari* (bitters), however I declare, without much conviction: *Not bad!*

At last, Copenhagen comes into view; the train enters the station on platform seven.

From the platform, we can see, further down, the main hall and a large illuminated sign indicating SAS, Scandinavian Airlines. But from where we are, we can't see the staircase to the main hall. Bodil quickly walks to the left, we follow her in single file, but no exit is in sight, so, when we are at the very end, at platform 20, I suggest: *Bodil, in my opinion, the exit is near platform one, that is, the other way.*

We go back to platform one... and of course the staircase is there.

As soon as we enter the hall, Bodil rushes to the offices at the bottom, saying: *I'm going to ask for information at the SAS desk;* I am puzzled because, from what I could understand, the SAS offices were on the first floor, while Bodil entered the post office buildings on the ground floor. She comes back disappointed, and I tell her that the SAS offices are upstairs. She runs up the stairs.

Anna Jole says nothing and looks at us helplessly, she obviously doesn't know how to behave, and again I ask myself: *Whatever is she thinking?*

Bodil comes back out of breath, it's 4.15 p.m.: *You have to take a taxi and run...* exactly what we already knew.

We hug Bodil in a hurry as we get into the cab. At the airport we run and run towards the gate... just to hear them informing us calmly: *Sorry the gate is closed.* The 5.00 p.m. flight is the last one of the day to Milan. I wonder if a triangulation is possible, maybe via Frankfurt, however the clerk looks at the ticket and says that with our fare the only possibility he can offer us is the flight for the next day, at nine o'clock in the morning. I look at Anna Jole and say: *I'm sorry, maybe you can call Einar to explain what has happened, we've done everything possible.*

We go out and ask the taxi driver to take us to the nearest hotel; five minutes later we enter the Dan Hotel.

We head towards the reception, but after a few steps Bodil runs to meet us, saying: *How nice, you are here too.* Both Anna Jole and I are amazed and speechless... *What on earth is Bodil doing here?* and without planning this in advance! How did she know we would miss the plane and which hotel we would choose? An accident or... Observing her a little better, I see that she has a big bruise near her left eye, and I also notice she has tried to cover up a large hematoma just under her eyebrow with make-up.

She drags us to a discreet corner and tells us that her husband is an alcoholic; he's in one of the hotel rooms. She had left Odense to bring him home. The man is difficult; under the influence of alcohol he beats her. We ask her if we can do something, she reassures us saying that she had already asked Alcoholics Anonymous for help, she was waiting for them to arrive.

Anyway, you're husband and wife, you have to get a double bedroom and make the most of it... and she goes to the reception.

I'm embarrassed, and so is Anna Jole: it's okay that the Danes are liberal but...

I watch Anna Jole, she's seriously worried and motions a clear 'no' with a nod of her head. I approach the reception desk with our documents and, despite Bodil's protests I ask for two rooms.

We tell Bodil that we're going to rest, we'll come down later for dinner at the restaurant, and we would be glad to have her as our guest.

She replies that she doesn't know if she can, but asks us to call her in room 225 around 7.00 p.m. Before going down, I try to call, a male voice replies, clearly altered by alcohol. I hang up.

The Dan's restaurant is nice, cleverly lit by soft lights and candles. Anna Jole asks me if Bodil is going to come, I reply I don't know; I tell her about the phone call, and I tell her that, if Bodil wants, she knows how and where to find us. We talk about ourselves, she tells me a little bit about her life and I do the same. As time goes by, the talk becomes more personal and I give her a fairly complete report about the history and the objectives of the *CEJH* (*Communauté Européenne des Jeunes de l'Horticulture*) and the *GFA Association of Giovani Florovivaisti Associati*, set up about ten years earlier by Cesare Bonomini, Celestino Miola and myself. I invite her to join and she says yes. I don't know it yet, but Anna Jole will become one of the Association's most precious resources and will keep the group of young people cohesive and energetic for years.

We go to bed fairly early; the next morning the 9 a.m. plane brings us back to Milan.

During the flight Anna Jole asks me if we'll see Bodil again, if she has solved her problems... I reply: *Who knows, maybe...*

In Milan, waiting for Anna Jole at arrivals, is Prospero, her boyfriend: they will get married and have children... but of course I only know this later. There's no one waiting for me, but before leaving, Anna Jole, embracing me, says: *You were a good husband... thank you;* and then: *She was really freaky, but what made me feel good was your tranquillity and the way you dealt with all that nonsense in such a quiet and serene way... as if it was the most natural thing in the world...*

I reply: *There's nothing wrong, every now and then, in relying on random events that aren't really random, what has to be... is; and anyway – equals attract.*

Anna Jole looks at me with big eyes, reflects a moment and then: *That woman was crazy, so if equals attract... what does that say about us...?*

I smile, I blow her a kiss and I walk on.

With Anna Jole, Anna Maria and many other women I have never tried to go beyond pure and disinterested friendship. Once Gabriella Lantero (The lady in purple) told me: *Among lovers, sooner or later love ends, friendship does not; you can confess things to a friend that you would never tell a lover.*

A purpose.
Now I have a purpose

I want to write a book, I don't want Francesca's life to be forgotten. I want to remember every moment I lived with her. It is said that: *A life that is not written is not honoured.* I want to honour her memory... to a certain extent I want her memory to be fixed in time...
I can't and don't want to forget her... she's a part of me and now I am desperately alone.
I don't know how I freed myself from religious symbols, and I don't even know if I've actually got rid of them. Holy water will wash away all the evil things, where did I hear this? In fact, they're preparing me for my last trial. They'll take me to the mountain top of the Foundation, the president will be seated at the summit, holy water will flow from the top straight from the president, it will drench all those in the lower levels and will wash away the ills and sins in each of us. I have the privilege of being placed very high, immediately below the level of the president's stalwarts. Water flows abundantly, it almost stifles my breathing, I can't even see properly. Suddenly I have a revelation, the president is pissing on everyone, and we suckers, are drinking his lies.

To hell with everything
I begin to write the book, sheet after sheet, draft after draft. The fact that in the book I leave open the fundamental questions that man has been asking since time immemorial, doesn't mean that I'm not a believer, but doesn't exclude the opposite either. I have simply come to understand that the indefinable can't be defined; defining it means to give it boundaries and therefore limits. So, how can we define being? And above all, why should it be defined?

Everything becomes confusing until suddenly Katrin Or says: *We've done everything we can for you here, so we've decided to send you home; since you've left your wife, we'll send you to your house in Mocomero. A special team chosen by me will accompany you and a group of people will remain to assist you for as long as you need.*

Those houses of Mocomero Valtolla

Las preguntas que no se responden por sí solas nunca tendrán respuesta.
(Questions that are not answered by themselves will never be answered.)

It's not easy to describe everything that happened, because I don't even know the whole story, I'll start by writing what I know.

Those houses, there in Mocomero Val Tolla, have names: starting from the bottom, the first is called *Casa Maria* (Mary's house), in memory and in honour of my grandmother. That's where my mother and most of her brothers were born. My grandfather Giuseppe was the son of a tailor from the Vigoleno area, who had found a small farm in Mocomero and moved there.

My great-grandmother was called Rosa Astorri. Apparently her parents had intended her to marry another man, but at the altar she said no and married Giovanni, my grandfather's father, instead.

Grandfather Giuseppe was a peculiar man; he used to go round taking peoples' measurements for new clothes; yes, clothes were tailor-made then and it is said that they used to spread ashes on the floor, getting the customer to lay down in them so as to take their measurements more comfortably! To make ends meet, he also acted as a middle man and sold whatever he could get, in short, the code word was *opportunist*.

He had a very beautiful pair of oxen, but they were from the plains: in the mountains, they needed rustic oxen, with strong hooves.

A peculiarity of the plains' oxen was their slightly reddish bottom. Giuseppe didn't lose heart, he bought a tin of black shoe polish and changed the colour of the hair on the oxen's back with a brush, then sold them as mountain ones. After five or six months it was reported that the hair of these oxen had changed colour, but by then it was too late.

When he realised that the family was too large, he decided to build a new house nearby and the old one was turned into a stable and farmhouse. One night the stable burnt down, but they managed to save the oxen and the cows. The roof burned, but it was rebuilt together with part of the walls on the upper floor. The walls on the ground floor remained intact.

Uncle Arturo was a partisan, *nom de guerre* Macario, *Aquila* (Eagle) Brigade; he died, after months of suffering, when he was only 21 because of a mortar splinter in his back: he always dreamt of buying a motorbike. He and uncle Primo cut down a large chestnut tree that became the load bearing beam of the floor. That beam is still there, and I didn't want it removed, now it pierces the bathroom wall and it's still there, as it was then, where they had put it.

From that fire, even if scorched, two more beams were saved and reused; I have preserved them. One supports small porch roof at the entrance, the other is the central beam in the *Casa delle Stelle* (House of Stars). I have also kept the floor tiles that paved the entrance to the well. The well is ten metres deep: my grandfather had his children build it, it was not there before.

Both cousin Gabriele and I went down it to clean it: Gabriele was motivated by the fact that he had been told that someone had thrown some weapons down there (they had not). There was just a piece of the so-called wolf, a tool used to recover the buckets that fell to the bottom. The water comes from a small spring about five metres deep. Now the well is also served by the gutters and drain pipe.

A couple of things have been saved from this house, the huge cooking pot, the table (the one in the attic). In wartime my grandfather used to attach the salamis horizontally under the table. One evening the Germans arrived, threw their weapons on the table, and asked for food. They didn't find the salamis that were right under their noses; my grandfather had bandaged his head (there was nothing wrong with it) and put himself to bed in order to avoid beatings.

In the end they left with our only sheep. There's still a knife and fork from the SS in the house, together with the harnesses for the oxen, one of which is broken, and – unless it's been thrown away – even a bayonet. The machine for bottling wine made by uncle Primo and the *travasa* – a huge wooden bowl made from a single piece of chestnut, are also still there.

The second house is called *Casa Celesta* (Celesta's House), because Celesta Groppi lived there, she rented it from the owners, called Rovellini. I remember Celesta standing there at the door.

As a child I had tuberculosis in my right lung and because I was too small to go to hospital, I was treated at home. Someone had to give me injections twice a day and aunt Lina was the family expert.

This is why my mother moved back to her birthplace in Mocomero for a while. I don't remember much about that time, but those injections, together with the x-rays, which, in those days were often used inappropriately, saved my life; however... I had a very high price to pay...

When I saw aunt Lina coming, I ran away, and it took hours to find me; those penicillin injections really hurt and my buttocks were punctured by about a hundred needles.

The sun burnt in the summer and the road was dusty, but that big woman was always there with a handkerchief on her head and a smile that stretched from ear to ear. Celesta was a good woman, she looked out for me, she was not afraid of catching it and she was always trying to make me eat something, even though I didn't have much appetite.

Just inside the door, on the left, there was a fireplace without a chimney, and the smoke damage on the stones outside can still be seen today.

There were also two small windows that I kept; one from the front of the house. Giovanni *dal masér (*the Sharecropper*),* a neighbour, used to put his arm through it from outside and tried to grope for a bottle of wine. I think Celesta knew and let him do it anyway.

One of the Rovellini boys, when he suggested I buy the houses, told me that in wartime they were hungry: one day they discovered a hole in the wall from which wheat grains appeared; they widened the hole and from time to time took some of this wheat that flowed from the room next door which was part of Giovanni's house. He used the house to store wheat, salami, etc. in the winter.

In the seventies this house was rented to Angela, together with *Casa Baccini*, she used to keep her salamis and cured hams there. It was also the *topaia* (clubhouse) because the youngsters of that time came down here to play cards, to eat, to listen to music at full blast...

The third house is the *Ernesta* or *Casa Lunga* (Ernesta's House, or Long House), partly as it's narrow and deep, and partly as it belonged to Giovanni Conti, nicknamed *Il Lungo* (the Long) because of his height. They say that as a young man he was a pain; but he never was with me. It was him who told me how – when he was ten, they restored the house and moved a very large oak beam (that beam is now above the fireplace in *Casa Baccini*). He also explained why there were stones protruding here and there from the outer walls. He told me that when families became numerous they simply 'stretched' the house, adding another piece on. Of course, this did not always please the neighbours, especially if they had windows, so those stones protruding from the wall indicated the vertical boundary. In this way, the owner prevented their neighbours from encroaching on their space. I sometimes call it *Casa Ernesta* because in the 1930s someone called Ernesta also lived there.

In the post-war period, Giovanni the Long rented this house to his brother Antonio who had just married Maria; their children, Lino and Rosa were conceived and born here.

The fourth house is *Casa Baccini* (Baccini's House): I don't know anything about them, and neither does anyone else from Mocomero. Our cousin, Maria from Mignano, lived in that house and it was she who told me, during her last visit that this was the Baccini's house even though I bought it from the Rovellini family.
Maria was over seventy years old and when I asked her why she called her house the *Casa Baccini*, she replied that she did not know, she simply told me that that was how it was known when she was little. Maria was very excited when she visited, she told me that she had spent the best years of her life inside that house and that she was happy that 'her house' would continue to live on.

The fifth house is the aforementioned *Casa delle Stelle* (House of the stars); nobody has ever lived in the front part of this house. It was built as a barn and shelter by my grandfather who exchanged it, I do not know for what, with the Croci-Castellana's who lived in the United States. He was a surveyor and he sold it on to the Rovellini-Groppi's, who, in turn, sold it to me. They used the money to buy the first truck for the Franzini company.

In the House of the Stars there are two paintings, a Batik illustrating Buddha day in Kandy which I brought from Sri Lanka. When I hung up that picture, Luca, the nephew, helped me, even though he was only a child; that painting fell on his head more than once, he still reminds me about it today.

Pier Paderni painted the other picture especially for that house. The name, *Casa delle Stelle*, derives from the fact that it has more than one storey and so the house is very tall.

Attached to the fourth house there is actually another one (where I have my study and the garage) and which was owned by the Curia. That house was inhabited by people who cultivated church land, and the priest of Castelletto.

I know of a certain Pietro who lived there until he moved to Carpaneto: for many years he kept saying that in summer you couldn't sleep anywhere as well as in Mocomero, and that he dreamt every day about the fresh air of Mount Vidalta.

So in short: *Casa Maria* was family property, now it is mine even if it is not registered as such, because in exchange I sold part of the flat in Piacenza to my sister.

Casa Celesta, Casa Baccini and *House of the Stars*: I bought all of them from the Rovellini; I was alone in signing the deed on my side, they were eleven – the judge who was nonetheless acquainted with this type of situation was still surprised. I bought *Casa Ernesta* (or the House of Giovanni the Long) from Pino, his son. I paid what he asked for without any discussion, after all it was right in the middle.

The last one that belonged to the Church and which is now part of the House of the Stars, was the most difficult to buy, even if it was the one that cost the least. My uncle Don Natale asked on my behalf. I wrote to the Curia, the parish inspector came to examine the situation. In the end I went to the Curia in person and spoke with Monsigneur Bozzuffi. I made him an offer, then a higher one, he asked me for a bit more.

The deed was finally signed, and they also gave me two more pieces of land; one no longer exists because the road passes over it, the other is on the other side of the road and borders *Casa Gogni* (House of Pigs, where I keep my archives) and the Inzani plot, which I bought together with Adriano, my brother in law.

Further back in time

The origins of *Case Maria, Casa Celesta*, the House of the Long (or Ernesta) and *Casa Baccini* go back a long way; they are registered in the Napoleonic land registry of 1850, but they had already been there for a long time — not as we know them today, however, as they've been rebuilt and probably extended many times on the same spot and with the same stones.

The oldest documented place names in Val Tolla (now Val d'Arda), all prior to 500 A.D., are: Mignano, Settesorelle and Mocomero, all the other towns and cities came later.

According to the latest research recorded by Angelo Carzaniga in the *Quaderni della Val Tolla* n. 9: *I have never come across an etymological hypothesis of the toponym Macomero; it does not sound either Latin or Germanic and is atypical for this area. Apart from a few cases, found recurring in the papers of S. Antonino, in hundreds of other documents the place is called and written Machomeria, which seems to be straightforwardly Greek, an unaltered transcription of the Greek machomeria, plural of the neutral machomerion, a noun which comes from the verb machomai, which means to combat, to fight a duel, to struggle. With the addition of the suffix 'erion', as found in words like sferisterio, (a place for playing ball), cimiterio (cemetery) etc., Machomeria assumes the meaning of 'place destined, or reserved, for fighting'.*

Because it ends in an 'a', and as the neutral gender had fallen into disuse, the ancient lawyers and scribes invariably interpreted the name Machomeria as being in the feminine singular, but subconsciously its true origins must have remained in local tradition, since in the sixteenth-century Estimates it is written: *In territorio Machomeriæ ubi dicitur ad Machomerias* (in the territory of Macomeria which is known as 'le Macomerie'), where the female plural in Latin recreates the neutral plural in Greek.

Macomero, therefore, would have had gymnasiums, or more simply perhaps fenced off areas or arenas where the Byzantine Supreme Commanders militia, during the wars against the Goths and the Lombards, could practise, or enjoy themselves in duels and wrestling competitions. Macomero was right at the entrance, where no one could pass unchecked.

In the article: *In casale Nerviano, Lugagnano, Mocomeria, Aminiano, Locas Montanas. Uomini, affari, nomi e luoghi al tempo dei Franchi.* (In the hamlets of Nerviano, Lugagnano, Mocomeria, Aminiano, Locas Montanas: Men, business, names and places at the time of the Franks) Angelo Carzaniga speaks of an act written in: *Macomero in April 886, the sixth year of Charles the Emperor, by Ariperto, a notary, and which records the division of assets agreed between Gaidoaldo son of the late Teodoaldo of Mocomeria on one side and Giovanni, Stadeverto, Leoperto and Veneroso, all brothers and sons of the late Lupone of Aminiano on the other.*

It would seem that Gaidoaldo did not keep to the decisions reached in previous judgements regarding the division of certain common properties in Macomero and Pietro of Niviano *Spolentino e sculdascio* (travelling financial administrator) denounced his improper conduct.

(Lupo, also called *Lupone*, was related to Teodoaldo, Gaidoaldo's father, and to Pietro's mother or father – we don't know).

Following a fresh judgement, Gaidoaldo guaranteed to give Pietro eight plots of land, a perch – an ancient Roman measurement, approx. ten feet) of vineyards adjacent to that of the same Pietro, and half a *iugero* (an ancient measure of land that could be ploughed by a pair of oxen in one day, approx. 120 x 240 feet) of arable land. He was also to divide up other common goods of Macomero in a regular fashion.

From various documents one can see that Gaidoaldo and his family were esteemed and respected in Mocomero and the surrounding area but as often happens among relatives in the dividing up their heritage...

Gaidoaldo took the highest ground (Monte) and from his name derives the term Vidalta. The houses of Mocomero in those times were covered with shingles and were certainly of very poor construction. Just uphill from Macomero, near Aminiano, where the artificial dam stands today, stood a large natural barrier, higher than the current concrete wall. That natural dam must have collapsed, after millennia of resistance, towards the end of the eighteenth century, since in 1805 Captain Boccia in his Journey to the Mountains of Piacenza noted to his great surprise and disappointment at not having found the famous walls of Mignano that he had admired in his youth, and of which only the stumps remained on both sides.

The Church of San Lorenzo

Mocomero had its church, now not far from the cement works, in the place known as the Small Island. The cemetery was also there. During the construction of the road some ancient tombs were discovered, some from the Lombard period. The Church of San Lorenzo was closed by the Bishop around 1500 because it had been abandoned, and it's possible that strange rituals were being performed there.

The inhabitants of *Casa Maria, Casa Celesta, Casa Ernesta* and *Casa Baccini*

Since 886 A.D., hundreds of people have lived in those houses. We know little or nothing about them; occasionally names are noted in registers or deeds of the time. Apart from a couple of solicitors, the majority were farmers who each had two rooms, one for the day and one for the night. And there they brought into the world their children, five to ten per family. When these children got married, they would leave home, some moved to other houses in Mocomero, others elsewhere.

There is no record of any violence occurring in these houses, even in times of war. Poverty, if by that we mean the lack of what we consider important today, yes, that was present. Hunger was sometimes there too, in wartime, for example, or when crops failed.

In the room where I sleep about 35 people have died, but more than 65 were born. Then this rhythm was a normal thing, like the seasons. Today it is no longer like that, there are some people already dead before they're born, today everyone's at each others' throat, if you don't HAVE, you are irrelevant, so we learn from the TV.

Well, now the fun begins!

I didn't need those houses, I was not even that interested, and this is the truth but... the Rovellini insisted on selling them to me.

I talked to my mother who was inclined not to buy them: *What will you do with them?* However, the price was low, something like €3,500 today, maybe they would have ended up in the hands of someone who would have then either adjoined our house or one of our plots of land in front of the house, on a downhill but sunny slope.

This was only the start, because then I bought Giovanni the Long's house; Pino wanted to sell it and insisted, he was in the middle of *Casa Celesta* and *Casa Baccini*; in the end, I bought it but it was more expensive. I paid him 7,500 euros paid over three years without interest (not being in a hurry and with devaluation I saved about 25%). At this stage, I couldn't begin to think of restructuring or of demolishing everything to enlarge the house where I used to live with my mother, without also buying the Church house, and so I closed the circle.

Many years passed, in my mind there were always two opposing possibilities, to demolish everything or to renovate everything.

In the end I think I chose the more illogical of the two (renovating) for reasons that I can only partially explain.

I know what convinced me to renovate those houses, but certainly it wasn't just for this: surely there was something telling me: *Don't destroy what many have built over so many years.*

The other was Gabriele. Gabri had just finished studying to be a surveyor and was working as an assistant to the architect Moresi. Maybe, if I entrusted him with the task of planning the renovation, I could help him in his career. If he did well, which I was sure he would, those houses would be good for his cv.

Gabriele was excellent at his job, without too many explanations, he understood at once what I wanted and, above all, wherever possible he used what was already there, nothing reusable was thrown away, because every stone, every beam was a piece of history.

In the end, this experience didn't actually help him, as Gabriele decided to change his career.

So far it has been more or less what really happened

Facts are facts, but behind facts are decisions and it's not always easy to work out why you make certain choices and the real motives are not always at a conscious level. However, there was a woman I loved and love more than myself. All this work, all my life, my every thought has been and is for her. I married that woman before God (if there is one), but it was a one-way thing. In the walls of that house there is the cry of a new-born baby, there is the moan of pleasure, smiles, tears and... the last breath.

Not all those who have lived there have gone away, if you touch the walls, if you look with your heart and mind, you can still feel them, something of them is still there, their dreams, their hopes. She is still there too, and the fact that she was only there a few times does not limit her presence.

And for the moment, I am always there too, even when I'm far away, keeper of houses and memories.

Merlin and the future

(Merlin may derive from the ancient Celtic Emryis Merydduin which perhaps meant Arturo; it is possible that Merlin was the bastard brother of King Arthur.)

You can perceive the future, however to look ahead also means taking responsibility for creating the future.

I can do this for myself, I DON'T WANT TO DO IT FOR OTHERS, I perceive it, but I DON'T WANT TO BRING IT INTO BEING.

To a large extent I wrote what I had to say in a poem that I published long ago in the book *Ali* (Wings). That summer in Monteisola it was the most read, the most played, it was broadcast on radio and television. Thanks to that poem the painter Danilo Manenti did a portrait of me, with the first verses as an inscription.

However, Danilo had a mischievous streak, he painted me with my hat at a rakish angle and... with the feather of an 'amberjack hen' (his words). That portrait is now in *Casa Baccini*.

That was only the first part (I wrote it in *Casa Baccini*).

The last part I wrote some time later, and the only person who read it almost immediately was aunt Genoveffa. The first part was well-liked, but I doubt whether many people really understood what

I wrote, in the same way that I doubt that they will understand the latter.

However here it is, in full.

Merlin

Sunrise and dew put to the sword.
Dreams of glory in the history books.
Fast the steed as thought.
Fly Merlin, ahead of time,
hide your anguish from yourself.
The pink door, the blue door, you will have to choose.
But there is no mind and there is no magic that opens the way for you,
that shows you the way.

> *Fly Merlin*
> *Fly through time*
> *hide your anguish*
> *from yourself*
> *after having loved so much,*
> *there is despair*
> *throughout creation.*
> *Escape far*
> *from time and glory,*
> *but you can't erase*
> *your memory.*
> *There is no more time*
> *there is no more mystery*
> *now that you have raised*
> *the last veil.*
> *Now that you no longer have identity*
> *you are ready for eternity*

Conclusions

Las preguntas que no se responden por sí solas nunca tendrán respuesta. Again: (Questions not answered by themselves will never be answered.)

I can actually say that there are many ways of dying; what I know for sure is that the physical one is the least painful.

I've never been too close to things. Maybe, the problem is that I can't forget, yet writing helps me to free myself from myself, from the pain and bitterness I have inside. Surely, there is a madness in my life, but I have always followed my instinct — the only thing that has never betrayed me. I regret nothing, in all my life I have always tried to allow others to be what they want to be, even against my will and my better judgement, even against myself.

I don't know what the future holds for those houses; if I find someone willing to pay the right price, I will sell them, otherwise it will be up to those who inherit them.

P.S.: *For the world as we know it today, I was born 'poor', as were my grandparents and my parents, but unlike them, I didn't know it; therefore, I never suffered from that poverty. Actually, I had everything I needed, I grew up with tea sent from London and a fair amount of powdered milk from the Marshall Plan that my uncle Don Natale used to bring to Levori, where I was born; I had poor clothes but I could almost always find the 30 lira each week to buy my Pecos Bill comics. Sometimes I gave someone the money to buy the comic at Lugagnano market on Friday. Other times I went alone Bore to buy the latest edition (walking to Bore from Levori and back took half a day). Pecos Bill fuelled my imagination, and up there, between the valley and the hills, I was living the adventures of that brave hero. I discovered all of this many years later, as well as the luck I had in being born at Levori. That valley, those mountains, with the natural cycle of the seasons, of life, of growth and of death, accompanied, trained and educated me in the first years of my life. This is why my mind has few constraints, and why I can think unconditionally and freely.*

The second part of the story

The second part of this story is the one concerning me more directly and is the one that Anna Prati Zani, a dear friend from Vezzolacca, encouraged me to write.

I was born in the hamlet of Levori, on the road that goes from Castelletto to Bravi and Vezzolacca, in the shadow of the ancient Church of Sant'Andrea. I have already written something about my childhood, what remains are moments, feelings that can't be put to paper. These emotions, like the colour of light, the movement of the wind, are something familiar; the valley is like a second womb that took care of me in those years.

It was the beginning of the post-war period and work was important; my father went digging for stones for the cement works on Mount Vidalta; besides being hard work, there were also night shifts and early wake up calls long before dawn. I remember voices, noises in the low candle light and the lantern. Electricity would be soon brought to the house, likewise indoor water that my mother desperately wanted: it was a great achievement.

The radio also arrives, placed high, above the fireplace, playing the songs of the Sanremo Festival and Claudio Villa.

Also, one evening the ballpoint pen appears, brought by a street vendor: after a glass of wine he forgot a whole box at our house. He noticed it when he got to Vezzolacca and returned to pick them up that same night. In Castelletto, television arrived in the mid-sixties and there were two, one in Cirillo's bar and one in the Rectory hall. Cirillo allowed us children to watch the evening programs until the end of the news: Carosello was already considered a programme for adults. Don Antonio allowed us to watch television on Sunday from 17.30 to 18.30 and the children's favourite series were the *Black Arrow* and *Ivanhoe*, whom we only identified as Roger Moore many years later.

There is a whole gallery of characters in my memory, faces that appear smiling and incredibly clear, pieces of life that remain inside me and that I have carried with me through time and forever. My teacher was Nicetta Canali, she hasn't changed so much 50 years later; there was also Anna, *la pavese* (from Pavia) but she could not, despite being good, be as nice as Nicetta.

There was a lot of confusion when I found a loaded machine gun in an old house in Castelletto; after disassembling it my father threw a part of it in the well and a piece on to the roof of the house, it was there until the house was demolished.

The tobacco of old Viceinz was bitter, and chewing left a bad taste in your mouth.

There was old Celesta *ad Granein*, who had snuff instead; if I think about her, I can still conjure up her peculiar smell that derived from the mixture of sweat and tobacco.

One day, when I was ten years old, my mother asked me what I thought about moving to Mocomero. My grandfather was alone there, and Mocomero was much closer to the cement works, so my father could get to work in ten minutes. I answered yes, and so that autumn we loaded our things on to a cart, closing the door of the house that had seen the birth of both me and my sister.

I finished fifth grade in Mocomero, in the old school that my mother had attended; it obstinately refused to fall down. I took my exams in Vernasca on a sunny day, going there on foot, walking along the ancient paths through the forest with my companions.

At home we often talked about what I would do *when I grew up*, whether to carry on studying or to start work. I had wanted to be a journalist since I was six or seven. I think this obsession came from the movie *Call Northside 777* in which James Stewart played the 'good journalist' who eventually made Truth triumph. Many years later I was to discover that their commitment is not always so noble; however I have always tried to carry out my journalistic work in the most honest possible way and without taking advantage of the power that derives from knowledge of the facts.

I was fourteen years old and it was the last year of secondary school; that morning in the winter, like every other morning, the bus took me to school and I watched the world go by through the fogged-up window. I saw Lino, who was a year older than me, and who was working as an apprentice mechanic. He was standing at the petrol pump, wearing the classic blue overalls, covered with oil stains, rubbing his hands, already black at 7.30 a.m., jumping up and down as he filled the tank of a car with petrol to keep off the cold. It was a decisive moment – I said to myself: *Whatever I end up doing, I'm not going to live like that.*

At the end of spring, my uncle Don Natale arrived at Mocomero and informed us that he had spoken with the director of the Provincial Agrarian Consortium of Piacenza and that there was the possibility of my obtaining a scholarship for the Minoprio School. The school had just opened, but was to be important, specialising in flowers, vegetables and fruit growing and gardening. That summer my father took me by train to Minoprio, in the province of Como. I had to sit an admission exam.

The first person I met was Peter Conti from Zurich who spoke Italian in a strange way, while I tried talking to him in French.
I also remember the interview with the horticulture professor, Philip Pasche, and that together with a group of boys, he made me pull up the grass in a flowerbed, explaining that I had to pull up all the roots as well, otherwise it would soon grow again. He asked me if I thought that school was important: I remembered Lino at the gas station and I managed to convince him that school was essential for me, so much so that I was one of the 40 chosen out of the 140 who applied. Minoprio School worked on a continuous cycle, one month holiday a year, a week at Christmas and one at Easter, half day lessons in the classroom and half a day working in the nurseries and greenhouses. The new park was built by my class, the rock borders were all laid by me.
It was not difficult if you enjoyed it and even if I was not 100% enthusiastic about it, I worked hard, because Minoprio cost a million and a half lire per year and my father's salary, earned from loading 50 kilo concrete bags onto trucks, was then 80,000 Lira a month. With those 80,000 Lira he had to keep himself, my mother, me and my sister going.

In the second year, during the holidays, I chose to attend a course at Hertfordshire College in St Albans, England. I learned a bit of

English mainly thanks to Slavic girls like Milka, Deni and Atena who worked in the kitchen. The principal, Mr. Eric Pelham, who also spoke French, was nicknamed 'pork chop'. I began to get to know London and the life of the Italian emigrants who lived there. My mother's brothers, Piero and Antonio, had a restaurant, the first in King Cross, the second in Greenford in Middlesex. Luigi, my father's brother, worked in a brewery and lived in a building on Gale Street. I went to England together with a black schoolmate from Somalia and on the return trip we took the wrong ferry; instead of docking at Calais we ended up in Boulogne sur Mer, not bad at all, but we had to wait seven hours for the first train to Basel.

At school I was the only student who visited *Commendatore* Enrico Sibilia, the former owner of the estate and the Villa Raimondi. If the School of Minoprio was to exist, it was down to the debts that the *Commendatore* had with the CARIPLO bank, to Ermanno Sozzi, another *Commendatore* and pioneer of Italian floriculture and to Giordano dell'Amore, president of Cariplo. *Commendatore* Sibilia came every day to see his orchids in greenhouse number 4. He always brought a brush with stiff bristles which he used to flick the ladybirds off the plants. In his villa he had a unique collection of books and sometimes he would talk to me about his youth and his many trips to Africa.

Professor Aureliano Brandolini, director of the Research Centre, caught me one day with a bulge under my jacket, but he didn't say anything, he knew very well that it was just some books that the old *Commendatore* had lent me.

Minoprio has never awarded another student with two medals for two first places: a gold one for being the best in the course and one for being the first in floriculture and gardening. The reason I got these medals is very simple: my need was much greater than that of my classmates.

When school finished I stayed in Minoprio for another year as a researcher at the CNR (National Research Council) but in practice I was the deputy head of the Floriculture section. At the end of 1970, Commendatore Ermanno Sozzi, flower grower and founder of the

School came to Minoprio; I really liked his Lamborghini and this man with a cigar permanently in his mouth attracted me, but I think he also liked me. One day he told me half in Milanese dialect and half in Italian: *The Communauté Européenne des Jeunes de l'Horticulture* (The European Organisation of Young Horticulturalists) *will meet in March in Baden Baden; they are young like you, why you don't go along, they will pay your travel expenses;* without needing to think about it, I immediately agreed. snowing heavily, and I wondered: *Will it be near Siberia?*

I met many boys and girls who were playing at being adults (and maybe they were a bit anyway); the president of the *CEJH*, youth section of *AIPH* (International Association of Horticultural Producers) was Rainer Laurehass from a flower nursery in Baden Baden; the deputy was Edmond Hollevoet, a grower from Belgium; the general secretary was Hans Peter Otto from Germany. There was also *Mrs Darling* (Freya Arlot), she was then the most beautiful florist in Fribourg (I saw her again many years later in Denmark, she had become unrecognisable, and for me it was a great disappointment), and Lucien Fevriero, a *Pied-noir* of Marseilles: we are still friends today.

Since Italy was not a member of the *CEJH*, I was allowed to pass for French to get my travel expenses paid. A few months later I went as an Italian delegate to the Floralies of Ghent in Belgium: there were other Italians there and my former classmates, Paolo Voltarel and Paolo Bellora.

Without realising it then, I came back really changed after those two journeys: the contact with other ways of thinking and living had broadened my mind. I understood this many years later, when I saw what happened with the young people I took with me: after a while their opinions broadened out and became less provincial. Here again, I was not more intelligent than the others, I was simply more open than others to communicate and to absorb different cultures, and this has changed me.

Management problems within the Association of Former Students of Minoprio School, which had been founded in the meantime meant that it was not possible to reimburse my travel expenses, so I did not attend the *CEJH* again until 1978, the year of the Søhus Congress in Denmark.

The person who instilled a passion in me for philosophy was Dr. Iancu Cabulea, a Romanian researcher at the André Mayer Foundation, who was studying the genetics of corn. Iancu and Socrates are the two masters who have had the most influence on me philosophically. I had been carrying out important research on gerbera flowers, working day and night, I myself took the measurements and carried out the analysis of variance with Basilio Borghi: the research was published under other names, with a simple thanks to the 'technician' at the end of the article.

A year later, despite my professor and superior Dr Baldi's opposition, the general manager Dr Giovanni Galizzi and Accountant Gastone Sturme, to keep within budget forecasts, had to let me go. I had begun to learn how politics works. Actually, it was an opportunity for me: in the following years I saw how the technicians at Minoprio were living comfortably, but outside the real world.

Waiting to do my military service, I started working with the Giacomo Bruni's company *Raites* that sold bulbs, seedlings and accessories for florists and growers. It lasted only four months, but was very intense, I met many people and many of the growers from Lombardy.

I also got to know the woman who would become my wife.

I had gone to Calco to sell some *Canna indica* to a grower. I arrived in that small town in my first car, a red Volkswagen Beetle bought second-hand from Caronti in Como; I was dressed in a black suit with a white shirt and a white polka-dotted red Pierre Cardin tie. Gina, the girl in the courtyard looked, at me curiously and I thought to myself: *This is a girl I could marry*; at that very moment, she said to her brother: *Mario, don't be taken in by anyone with a suitcase.*

I left for my military service on 24 September. They sent me to Verona to the 67th Legnano Infantry Regiment, V Territorial Autogruppo and 2nd Field Artillery Regiment. After the *CAR* — initial training period — they made me a 'Moviere', a sort of Military Traffic Controller. I realised that military service was a waste of time. Then one day while I was in hospital in Verona, the doctors confirmed that I had two inguinal hernias. The medical colonel asked me if I wanted to be operated on, I answered no so they sent me home for five months.

Where I come from, it is thought and said that a boy is allowed almost everything, but at the end of military service you stop being a boy and you become a man. At that point, there are two imperatives: 1) a permanent job and 2) a wife.

I tried for both. I returned to floriculture, but my permanent job wasn't really right for me, even if it was well paid. The owner, Venanzio Meroni, had a floriculture company in Pessano con Bornago and was a close friend of a former school mate of mine, Alberto Alberti. He loved good living, big cars, night clubs and women. He believed that everything was easy, and he was actually very lucky with the succulent plants he imported from the Edelman company in Holland: he was selling truck-loads throughout Italy; Alberto took a nice commission and Venanzio earned a lot of money. When I arrived, the relationship between Alberto and his girlfriend *Carlina* was almost over because the money side of things between them had never been clear; Alberto kept asking for more and more and he got fed up because actually he didn't have any money, but I would only find that out later.

It was a relatively quiet time, working all day in the greenhouses, travelling in the van to Milan and its surroundings to make deliveries, and once with Venanzio to Arma di Taggia to deliver geranium cuttings.

One day Venanzio showed me a diamond ring and told me: *It cost more than a million – I'm selling it for 250,000 Lire.*

I replied that I had no money and he said: *I can keep back 50,000 a month from your pay.*

I replied that I would consider it. Starting from the feast day of Saint Lucia, I was again in contact with the girl from Calco, Gina (Virginia); I was visiting her almost every Thursday. In my free time I was inventing floricultural gadgets; I created a humidifier for musk sticks, and Venanzio said: *This is worth following up, you put up the idea; I'll put up the capital.*

To be able to apply for the patent we formed a company, MC Ltd. In one spring we sold 1.5 million pieces; at a rough estimate, my share should have been about 45 million lire – at that time enough to buy a house. The problem was that Venanzio no longer had the money, he had used the MC funds to pay off the debts of his floricultural company; in fact, I discovered that he still owed around 100 million to the greenhouse builder.

The company's money was not enough to bale out the floricultural business, and a cheque issued by him bounced. The authorities made a mistake and called me to court in Bergamo; but it was easy for me to demonstrate that the signature was not mine; I had a statement from the bank stating that I was not a signatory to the account.
I quit my job and I had to get in a lawyer to be removed as an employee: they paid me 300,000 lire after three months, with a post-dated cheque.
It was at that moment that I decided to take some risks in my life.
I realised that it was not important what one had – it could be lost – it was more important what you could do; if you had the ability, you could rebuild everything, but to do so it was necessary to be: it was then that I decided to be myself.

I started from scratch as a salesman and trader in floriculture chemicals; soon I realised that the big multinationals only left me the small customers – they dealt with the big ones directly. It was therefore necessary to develop my own products.

I set up my own business and finally, in 1975, I set up the Flortecnica magazine with the aim of helping companies to grow.
I was well aware that the growers did not want products from me but *the knowledge of how to use them.*
I had made many acquaintances, the first Flormart professional exhibitions were held in Padua, the magazine was a way to reach all the nursery gardeners directly at home. The first issue was printed at Ceretti Graphics in Gorgonzola; the logo at the top was composed with wooden characters. The text was made with lead blocks and the photographs were zinc clichés. The pressure caused by the lead typeface is visible in those copies even today.
1977 was an important year, at least from a personal point of view –

I married that girl I had met seven years earlier, the one who I had judged as being: *Someone I could marry.*

In January 1978 I was on one of the islands in Sri-Lanka. I think that this trip was influenced by two books by Folco Quilici (*Giramare* and *Giraterra* – On the Seas and Around the Earth) because in Trincomalee the only cultivated flowers were those of the Oceanic Club. Bo Derek was there too, she was shooting Tarzan, 'the ape man'; but she soon put me off by having her hair combed while she was eating. In a village near Trincomalee, I would later meet the girl who would become my foster daughter. A few years later the war broke out between the Tamil tigers and the Sinhalese government; the bandits killed this girl's father. She had polio, and ended up in a refugee camp in Javna. I started sending her some money, 50,000 Lire at a time; for me it was nothing, for her it was a lot. She was able to complete her studies and become a teacher.

In 1979 I picked up my contacts with the *CEJH* (*Communauté Européennes des Jeunes de l'Horticulture*) and I participated with Cesare Bonomini, Paolo Voltarel and Celestino Miola at a conference held in the school in Søhus (Denmark). In that year Cesare, Celestino and I also went off to discover Paris, described as *A Moveable Feast* by Ernest Hemingway and the favourite city of Henri Miller and Anaïs Nin.
I also went for the first time to Leningrad (now known again as St. Petersburg) and to Moscow with Cesare and Giancarlo Residori.
I found Leningrad to be an aristocratic city of stunning beauty. On this occasion we were organising the first trip to the USSR for floriculturists in the following year (the same year as the Olympic Games).

In 1982 several meetings were organised with young floriculturists, the main ones were at the Bonafous Institute in Collegno and in Mocomero and finally the *GFA – Giovani Florovivaisti Associati* (Young Growers' Association) – was set up; I was the president, Cesare Bonomini vice-president and Celestino Miola secretary.
Year after year, the *GFA* attended various congresses in different European countries: Sweden (in 1982, I took the opportunity of

visiting the Arctic Circle, passing Uppsala, Haparanda, Rovanjemi, and then descending to Kalmar, Kuopio and, further south to Helsinki), Norway, Austria and finally, Germany.

In Vallecrosia, Liguria was my greatest friend, Ezio Troia; as a young man he had built the flower floats at A *Mar Parà*, participating in the Battle of the Flowers in Ventimiglia.

In 1984, with the aim of promoting the magazine Flortecnica, I organised the *Florum*, the first national floriculture symposium at the Grand Hotel del Mare in Bordighera. From that symposium, *Unaflor*, the National Union of Floricultural Companies would be set up. Also, in 1985, at Pschor Keller in Munich, with an attendance of 1800 young European nursery gardeners, I was elected president of the *CEJH*, headed at that time by three presidents with equal powers, one represented Northern Europe (the Swedish Boerie Ohlin), one represented the centre (the Belgian Paul Hollevoet) and I represented southern Europe; the general secretary was the German Jochen Winkoff.

It was the first time that an Italian was elected president of a body representing 12 countries and 15,000 young people of Europe.

In Munich I also met Heidi Tjelle, a Norwegian woman (at least I believed she was until five years later, I discovered she was German) who had lived for many years in Daytona, USA and who spoke an infinity of languages. With Heidi I would discover Norway in a unique and fantastic way, thousands of kilometres, fjord after fjord, trolls, Oelda, many fables and stories of life. Heidi has remained a dear friend.

I was travelling non-stop: people often called the Bad Hotel in Scheveningen, and the lady at the reception replied that Mr. Croci would be staying there at the end of the month; in fact, I was going to Holland almost every month, but — in those days — no one could speak or write about flowers without taking that country into account. Israel was also important; I think I've been there at least a dozen times.

In 1994 *Flormercati* commissioned me to organise a trip to Israel for their Council, about ten people in all. After a few days spent in Israel, the president of *Flormercati* exclaimed: *Arturo, you really know everyone here too.* How could I explain that wherever flowers were grown was my home.

Among the other non-European countries I have visited was also Zimbabwe, and my experiences there were the subject of the novel On the footsteps of Livingstone, as well as Kenya, Santo Domingo, Mexico, Argentina, Costa Rica, Chile, Bolivia, Colombia, Thailand, the United States, Abu Dhabi, Dubai, Australia, Japan etc.
Sometimes I was invited as a speaker to conferences, sometimes for a professional exhibition, sometimes simply to see how floriculture was developing in a given country.

I started publishing books almost by chance.
My greatest satisfaction is having contributed to the technical, scientific and historical education of many technicians and students, but also of many botanical enthusiasts and amateurs.

At the end of the 1990s, together with Pier Paderni, Adelio Gaviraghi and Dr Giacomo Tiraboschi, we made plans for the *Melaverde* television program. Finally, only Dr Tiraboschi continued to believe in it until, a few years later, one day he announced that the program would be shown on *Retequattro*. Tiraboschi gave me the task of writing the texts relating to the programmes about flowers and plants and then the discussions with Father Demetrio Patrini. Tiraboschi also introduced me to Silvio Berlusconi and I became his author, after television appearances as a 'gardener'.
My wife hated Silvio because I became completely absorbed in him. In fact, I always knew when I had to go to Arcore or Macherio but I never knew when I would come back. All this culminated in a large workshop organised by *Antologia*, named *Italia giardino d'Europa*. On that occasion I experienced being a presenter alongside the TV star Gabriella Carlucci.

How can I explain to people (and to my colleagues) that money was not my goal? For me this has always been the hardest thing, of course I need money and it is important to the extent that it allows me to do what I want, but for me money itself is something worthless. This way of thinking sometimes (often) landed me in trouble in the sense that I could not squander it because I had NO money to squander.

However, like most people in the Western world, I had a secret hope that suddenly a fertiliser, a book, and so on, might alleviate my chronic money problems.

This introduction is necessary to understand why my colleagues — Dr Aldo Colombo was the most insistent — were always yelling at me because I was wasting time in activities for which *I was not earning money*. In the autumn of 1995 I received a telephone call from a certain Augusto Landresi, a journalist at *Il Corriere della Salute*, then a supplement to *Corriere della Sera*. Landresi needed information on interior landscaping with plants, and he confessed he knew nothing about it. Finally, I gave him enough information to allow him to write his article, which came out some time later with a big thank you.

Naturally, I was reproached for having lost the afternoon in a non-productive job, such as helping students complete their theses etc. Actually, it is quite true, many of those people have vanished into thin air, but many graduates, especially Dr Silvia Scaramuzzi, consider me as a teacher.

About a year later, Landresi showed up again, asking if I was interested in working for a project outside my normal area, the answer was: *Before saying yes or no, I have to know what it is.*

I met Laura Stoppani, a woman who was going to become my super professor of editorial marketing, and the editing staff of De Agostini. I made plans to publish *Verdissimo*, a work in 100-weekly issues, including over 500 plants, which was completed in two years. *Verdissimo* had great commercial success in Italy, in Spain, and in Japan. We also started to publish another work, *Rose & Rose* but because of changes in the top management at De Agostini, the work was never completed.

In the late nineties, I also became the press manager for the professional exhibition Miflor, organised by FieraMilano. Later I worked on the Rome Fair for the Flòroma Business exhibition and then for Padovafiere for the Flormart/Miflor exhibition. I also prepared a project for a varietal fair for the Viareggio Flower Market, and I organised the Demetra exhibition for the City of Camaiore.

I have also helped various companies and cooperatives to overcome moments of crisis or better plan their future; how strange – the only future I never planned was my own. I received an invitation to attend a meeting of horticultural publishers (sic!) at Pèrols, in France. The 'HortiMedia Europe Association' was set up, and I was President in 1995-1996. In 2001 I organised the 'HortiMedia' meeting for the second time in Genoa on the occasion of *Euroflora*.

In the late 90s, Franco Locatelli and Wim van Meeuwen and I set up Grandparents' Day. The first promotional campaign for Grandparents' Day was made with the contribution of the European Union, the flower nurseries of *Unaflor* and the Dutch Flower Council. According to research from 2006, it seems that 70% of Italians knew about the existence of Grandparents' day, and that it takes place on 2 October.

In those same years, thanks to Franco Locatelli, I became the spokesperson for the three Italian professional organisations in the Plants and Flowers committee of Copa-Cogeca in Helsinki and this went on for a few years, with meetings in different countries of Europe. Later, in Angers, the three organisations began to express their different opinions, and *Unaflor* began to decline, so in 2000 I decided to withdraw from that position.

I would have continued indefinitely, I would never have stopped, I'm sure. It was impossible for me to change my life. In 2004, I experienced a disappointment that was new to me, I had forgotten that *the only one to whom you owe faith and trust is yourself...*
That year I had visited four continents in three months; in 2005 I made countless trips to Argentina, Holland, Germany, Switzerland, several times to Sicily, the last two in the November for *The open days in Marsala*, and in December for the *Garofano d'Argento* (Silver Carnation Awards). I got back from Giarre on 12 December. On 15 December 2005 at 8.15a.m. my aorta was dissected.

Back to Mocomero

The hospital in Bergamo prepared everything; they put me on an ambulance motor bike: I'd never seen one before. It's a very powerful bike but with a closed cockpit, the driver steering with the handlebars and, to one side, a comfortable seat for the passenger.

A large screen allows us to see the road. Two other escort vehicles follow us. It's a foggy afternoon but we should get there fast enough, in less than two hours. We don't, in fact; the fog gets thicker and the control panel with the navigation system is not clear, the driver is forced to slow down and to contact base regularly to get updates on our position. We should be near Lugagnano, I can't see anything, just the blue line on the navigator's screen. I tell the driver to leave the Arda river on the right and follow the straight road to the cement works. We are lost again and the driver stops. I take the wheel, slowly, following my instinct and trying to follow the line of the river. After the cement works and the abandoned Molino Teodoro (a mill), the fog disappears, now we are really close.

Mocomero had barely changed since I left; my houses are in sight and my heart beats furiously in my chest... how much time has passed... how many memories... all the people I've loved no longer living. It's true I wasn't born here, yet...

There's no one here, the lower part of the village is uninhabited, has been now for years... We enter by the garage door and there's my sister, with a basket under her arm; she looks at me calmly, unsurprised, as if it were normal, as if she had seen me yesterday...

I just have the strength to stutter: *Hello*, and her: *Hello! Matteo's around somewhere...* and she goes into my mother's house through the connecting door. I think that for her little has changed over the years and that her mind continues to live in a world of its own.

I open the door that leads to the staircase and I head for the bedroom... slowly I open the door, it's all exactly the same, just as Francesca and I had left it... I sense her presence in the walls, in the armchairs, in the objects... in the bed, my mind is faltering... my gaze is blurring with tears, my legs no longer support me... I'm trembling.

Leaning on the bed I make it to the armchair and I let myself fall...
with my eyes lost in nothingness.

In the meantime, the escort car arrives, Katrin doesn't enter, she
stops at the door, observes with half-closed eyes, without speaking;
in the end she whispers: *Now I know how much you loved her.*

I look at her and shes sees my sadness and endless pain, Katrin slowly
closes the door and leaves me with my memories.

My assistants, even if they're more like guards really, settle in the
guest room and in the neighbouring houses. There are four of them,
they almost never speak, they communicate with each other by
looks and gestures; later I discover that they also use telepathy.

Katrin, before returning to Bergamo, tells me: *Arturo, now you're in
your home, think about getting better and be at peace; Hadas, which
means 'flower' in Hebrew, will protect you and never lose sight of you,
it's for your own safety.*

Hadas is a strange character, he hardly speaks, and when he does his
voice is croaky, I can't see his face well, but I don't care. He hands me
a weapon, after pressing some keys, it looks like a gun, when I hold
it it lights up. Hadas says: *Now it's configured to your DNA, only you
can use it;* he shows me a key saying, *In this position you stun, in this
you kill, you have a hundred shots, then you have to change the charger.*

Hadas concludes: *Rest, I'll be outside the door, however if you call me,
I'll hear you even if I'm in another room.*

I remain alone, with an empty gaze and my mind immersed in
memories...Francesca... how many times have we made love here?
What's left of our life?

All great loves end sooner or later, as the Romans — and my friend,
Professor Giovanni Serra — used to say. Is this really true?

If it were really like that, why do I keep feeling her at my side?

But I can't hold her hand and I miss her.

Francesca... I close my eyes and let you into my imagination.

Francesca

How strange and extraordinary life is. Perhaps each one of us, without knowing, has a more or less conscious quest. We often believe that we make our own choices, or we think that what happens is completely random. There are also those who believe that what we are controlled by higher entities or the laws of attraction.

I don't know what the truth is, nor for what reason; what I am sure about is that things happen, maybe only inside ourselves but they happen; some are extraordinary and make us appreciate life more. In my case, a special meeting gave a sense and a reason to my existence. The turning point, or the conscious vision, happened on 15 December 2005. In the 15-20 minutes before the great darkness, I saw everything I had experienced in a flash. My inner dialogue was calm and initially emotionless, as if I were an external observer, impartial and indifferent. I told myself that after all I had been very lucky. Born into a good family, poor but... I didn't know it at the time and for this reason my childhood was happy and extraordinary, in the second natural womb of my little valley a free and unconquered valley, where nature in all its manifestations is the master. I had a good education, first in the valley, then in Minoprio, London, Barcelona and then... in many nations of the world.

And finally, I managed to deal with people and facts without getting involved too much. Some of these meetings could have led to power and wealth, but instinctively, I never deviated from my path. No, I had not accumulated wealth, but I was at peace with myself. So, I thought... *Maybe, my life can end here.*

Just then my emotions enveloped me in an indescribable sadness and pain, and endless longing... *It's a pity I didn't have a little more time to spend with friends and with HER.*

Yes, the last thought was for her. A few minutes before I had tried in vain to call her to tell her I was sick. She was travelling to work and her phone was off. The ambulance men ask me what happened, I speak of the pain in my chest, the pain in my arm, that I couldn't feel my left leg. My time is over... I slide, without realising it, into unconsciousness.

It was a sunny day and I was visiting a friend. This man talks endlessly and speaks to me in a chaotic way about his activities and his projects, how he's organising his office and company. He takes me to a room next to the house and lets me in. Inside, sitting at a desk, is a girl. The girl is smiling with big bright eyes, she's a sunny person. After so many years I still remember that moment and those deep eyes that have bewitched me ever since. She got up and held out her hand simply saying: *Nice to meet you, I'm Francesca.*

At that moment I wasn't really aware of the effect of her presence, and I couldn't imagine what my future would be with the most important woman in my life. The seed had nestled in my heart, even though I wasn't ready for it. I had other interests and other passions, but I also had a rather childish and selfish mentality. I as without malice or ulterior motives but, yes, a certain amount of self-importance.

After a while, I accidentally saw Francesca again. She was such a positive person and it was good to talk to her. Nothing more. Towards the end of 1987 together with Franco Locatelli, Giacomo Ustignani and others we set up the Miflor exhibition in Lacchiarella. In the afternoon, after the launch of the first Miflor exhibition by the Agriculture Minister, I was free to visit the various pavilions. I was more interested in the exhibitors of flowers and plants and a little less in the merchandise. The first person I meet is Francesca, from a distance she welcomes me with a smile and finally... a whole body warm and strong embrace... no one had ever hugged me that way, so intimately. That contact, unconsciously, linked me to her definitely.

I came back to see her on Saturday afternoon and Sunday morning. To save time and to better orientate myself, I climb the stairs and pass on to the balcony and already, waving, I think of her imminent hug.

In that same period, the relationship I had with Mafalda ended in a painful way. It was an intense but short relationship. It started in a taxi, on a spring evening between Netanya and Tel Aviv. In the hotel, as everyone got in the lift, she turned her key round discreetly, but looking me straight in the eye, showed me her room number.

Once in my room I was undecided whether to accept the invitation or not. After about ten minutes, I looked at myself in the bathroom mirror and said: *Go ahead but remember this will end in tears.*

So it was. They say that when things don't work out between two people, the responsibility should be shared evenly. Perhaps my greatest responsibility was to the mirror in Tel Aviv.

When I asked her why, her answer was: *I'm neither fish nor fowl.*

In one of the exhibition aisles, I see and speak briefly with Mafalda for the last time... She tells me very angrily: *You'd better grow up.*

I stare at her for a long time without looking away and I think: *At the cost to my self-esteem and dignity? No thanks.* I don't answer, I turn around and leave.

The way in which the story with Mafalda ended left me embittered and disheartened, so much so that I promised myself that I would never again allow myself to be involved so deeply with a woman. How wrong I was...

In the following years I was to see Francesca here and there and on my visits to companies. One day we talk about an exhibition in Rome. I'm going there by car and Francesca asks me if she can come with me, she'd like to be at the exhibition in the late afternoon to check that everything's in order before the opening.

I gladly agree to give her a lift and I go to pick her up. On that trip we talk all the way with just a quick stop for lunch. It's a pleasant and peaceful journey. I feel comfortable with Francesca, she knows how to listen, but it's also nice to listen to her opinions. I don't remember where the fair was, but we got there without noticing the time or the kilometres.

At the exhibition everyone gets on with what they have to do and then, a few hours later, a friend accompanies the group to the hotel where we're all staying. After dinner, we all go off together, wandering the centre of Rome in search of the famous Trevi Fountain. I had been there many years before, but in the daytime, and then I was still too young to appreciate its beauty fully. At night the fountain is even more suggestive and... it's one of the moments that are set in my memory... It was nice to admire it with Francesca by my side. Back in the hotel before going to bed I give her my room number in case she needs anything. I realise my mistake the moment the words are out of my mouth... She smiles at me and says: *No, It's okay.* In the following days we see little of each other and only in passing, she's busy with her work and I with mine. After the exhibition I go back home by myself, she with her colleagues.

We met each other casually several times after that. Once, I alluded to her physical appearance which is definitely not currently in fashion; she answered me calmly, but firmly: *You know, I'm well aware of my body's limits.*

I let the matter drop; I still didn't have the courage to talk to her openly, partly because I wasn't clear on a conscious level just what I felt for her. I couldn't explain why she seemed to be such a great beauty in my eyes and why she attracted me so much. In fact, she was the only woman with whom I have ever felt perfectly comfortable.

I'm invited to a big corporate event. I have to make a brief report for the company's customers. It's also a good opportunity for the company where Francesca works. I make my presentation, Francesca makes hers and everything goes well. The day after, we have to visit some contacts, in the evening after dinner, we go to bed. Together we climb the stairs of the hotel and then... something simple yet extraordinary happens, a kiss on the mouth that takes my breath away and turns me upside down. The world disappears; I feel a shiver running through my body to the depths of my soul. Breaking away is painful, I look into her eyes a little surprised, she replies with a serene and happy smile. We each go into our own rooms. Once in bed I don't know what to think, that kiss has triggered feelings and emotions never experienced before and that I can't control.

I can't sleep; then at one point, Francesca knocks on my door and enters the room... *To chat for a bit.* We talk about this and that, at some point we discuss the way choices should be made, was it better to make them in a logical, rational way, or to rely on our instincts. It wasn't long before our mouths found each other and then our hands too, she pretends to stop, gives and doesn't give, we're both very aroused but she doesn't allow me to go any further and at some point gets up and wishes me a good night.

Of course, I can't sleep, I try to reflect on what's happened but I can't find the answers to my inner questions. My plane leaves early in the morning and I have to get up at least two hours before. The whole hotel is still asleep. Before leaving the room, I look for a piece of paper and quickly write: *All my choices, I have always made with my heart.* When I pass Francesca's room, I slip the note under the door. While my companion takes me to the airport, I feel a deep longing. Leaving Francesca is painful, I would like to see her again, embrace her, kiss her and love her... again and again.

As soon as I land I try to call her... She's unreachable. I drive home and try again, no chance. A couple of hours later it's Francesca who calls me, she was out and about on company business... All's well, but I miss her. We meet again soon after and look for a suitable place to get together. She tells me that as soon as she got home, she left her other lover... She didn't want two lovers on the go at the same time. I felt an instinctive jealousy learning she had a lover, but I also told myself that I had no right to judge her behaviour and her choices. On the other hand, I really appreciated that she had left him for me. We talk for a long time and the windows steam up. Then our mouths and our hands search for each other, this time there is no resistance. We both want a lot more, but we aren't in the right place. We leave reluctantly, we both wanted our first time to be extraordinary and indeed it would be.

The occasion was an event on the Côte d'Azur, we made sure to book rooms in the same hotel. With my heart beating like crazy and overwhelmed with emotion, I knock on her door. Francesca is in her pyjamas, we're in each other's arms without uttering a word, her lips are inviting, her body even more. She looks at me disappointedly and says: *Bad luck, right now... I've got my period...* I don't care, and I let our bodies search for each other and merge. After making love we talk and talk, I want to know everything about her and she wants to know everything about me. In the morning we wake up in each other's arms, we have slept just a little, but we feel full of life.
Suddenly I realise that until then I had only had sex, this was the first time I had really made love. It's time for me to go back to my room and she comes with me. When she tries to get back into her room, she can't, the keys are inside, and the door has closed automatically behind her. No problem, Francesca goes down to the

reception in her pyjamas to get a passe-partout. From that moment on, we see each other as often as possible.

Our favourite place is in the countryside halfway between our respective homes. We call it 'the hare place' because one day, after we had made love, a hare appeared, looked at us and then ran away. We said to ourselves: *He's probably looking for his she-hare.* We look for any opportunity to meet up: Sanremo, Rome, Naples, Taormina and many other extraordinary places which, in my memory, are all connected to her.

Francesca often comes to see me in my valley, we make love in every possible place, in the woods, in the castle. Our body chemistry, at least for me, is extraordinary. Every time, after making love, I relax and tell her things and facts of my life that I have always kept to myself. With Francesca I'm not afraid to show my real self, all my strengths and weaknesses. She's patient and intelligently, slowly helps me to change my rougher aspects. With her I learn to listen, observe and be patient. Francesca writes me love letters, Francesca calls me, she's ready to leave her family and insists that I do the same with my wife and go and live with her. I reflect and I'm afraid to take that step, I keep telling her no. There were several reasons for my refusal; I didn't feel I could leave my wife after so many years together, even though we were no longer close; but there would also be repercussions for my work which was the most important thing in my life. Up until then my magazine was my life and nothing was more important. There was also another aspect that terrified me and that concerned Francesca. How would her children, the rest of her family, take it? They would certainly take it very badly. I was aware she was going to pay a very high price and I didn't want her to do this.

After some time, however, I realise that the most important thing in my life is no longer my magazine, my job, but it really is her... Francesca. I told her that I would do it, that I was ready to leave everything and go and live with her. She looked at me pensively and said nothing. We continued to see each other, even Francesca's way of loving has changed, she is no longer a child in love, she has become a woman in love.

Francesca doesn't use that word love very often, for her it's not to be trivialised, but when she says she loves me she penetrates the depths of my soul and always conquers me.

Francesca loves her children deeply and I know that they have priority, I understand. Once when talking about this, I ask her: *Do you really think I can love a woman who doesn't love her children?*

Mocomero becomes our home, my room becomes hers, my side of the bed becomes hers... every corner in the house speaks of her and the house now has a queen, always present... even when she's not physically there.

The coming dark age

The days and months pass by, I never leave my room. Hadas regularly brings me food on a tray, and, as far as he can, he tries to prise me out of the catatonic state I find myself in. He doesn't speak, but his thoughts still find their way to my brain; I'm too far from a state of awareness, I'm simply wandering through nothingness, but I listen, from a distance. Hadas tells me that Mocomero has changed a lot, that very few of the people I knew have stayed on. According to him, the new inhabitants aren't trustworthy.

My group of little houses, so he tells me, is known to the valley's inhabitants as *The castle of Forlanini* because of an ancient legend, and I can therefore use the title Count of Forlanini. It makes me laugh just thinking about it, I've always been allergic to honorific names. According to Hadas, I also have to be wary of my nephew, my return has upset his plans and according to him he's plotting to get rid of me.

Lugagnano has become a no man's land, ruled by the mafia, and where drug dealing is the most honest activity. It's no longer possible to go there without an armed escort, and never at night. The police and the law no longer exist, the service only functions − poorly − in large urban areas. The situation in the upper valley is no better; it's safer to travel by day, never alone and always with a weapon: now it's no longer a question of the old-style Brigands of Valtolla attacking the French who wanted to tax them, but robbers and killers of all kinds. All semblance of order and control has disappeared and only the law of the strongest is in force.

Hadas, before going out, always makes sure that the blaster is within my reach and that I know it is there. I've never used a weapon except on military service exercises, and I'm convinced that the best weapon is the brain and intelligence: violence can only generate more violence.

I think about what Hadas told me about my nephew: almost certainly, he was to blame for the death of my brother-in-law, who had never accepted his son's partner. I'm saddened by his loss, for me he was the brother I never had. Even if lost in nothingness, a part of me began to reflect and to think that Hadas could be right.

In the evening, while I'm half-asleep, I'm brooding, but my ears are alert and analyse every sound, from the wind whistling through the gaps in the building, to the house martins whose nest is under the roof tiles, to the woodworm that stop chewing at the slightest noise. Suddenly, I hear a noise that's unusual, I can't identify it, it's almost certainly coming from the study ceiling; it's as if someone was clinging with crampons to the wooden beams. Suddenly it springs to mind that someone is trying to get into my room from above. Whoever it is, they are certainly not coming to kiss me good night. I check the blaster, the selector is set to stun, I move to the darkest corner and strain my ears to identify the source of the noises getting closer. Instinctively, I stretch out my hand in the sound's direction and pull the trigger; I move my hand a few inches and press again, this time continuously. I hear two choked screams and the thud of someone falling. After a few seconds, the silence is broken by the sound of frenzied steps and from the noise, I assume it's my guard. The room lights up and Hadas enters with his weapon drawn; from my corner, next to the wardrobe, I inform him that everything's fine. Hadas simply says: *It was your nephew with his girlfriend, they tried to get to your room from the ceiling; their weapons, even if antiquated, had the selector on "kill". They both fell down the stairs head first and broke their necks. They are dead.*

I reply laconically: *Get rid of their bodies.*

I go and sit down emotionless, my mind blank.

The days pass, every now and then I hear the crack of the blasters, the guards' excited voices. One day Hadas enters my room and, for the first time, from his voice I hear that he's upset: *Look... we've already killed over fifty people who have tried to get in to steal stuff. Whether you're really the Count of Forlanini or not, use your power and give some instructions, we can't go on like this...*

In one way or another, his appeal hits home and shakes me out of my thoughts.

The next morning, I ask Hadas to take me downstairs. The men arrive and take me to *Casa Ernesta* in a sort of sedan.

Nothing has changed, the pictures and the photos are in place, on the wall going up to the stairs there's a poster of Tex Willer; it's strange, I don't remember hanging it up. In its place, there was a framed copy of the Wisconsin Evening News of 14 February 1929 with the news of the Valentine's Day massacre; who knows where that ended up.

Hadas informs me about my financial situation, that the lawyers want to talk to me about the settlement for my ex-wife and that it would be a good idea for me to have a maid to look after the house and do the cooking. I ask Hadas to look for women who might be suitable.

A few days later, Hadas organises a meeting with five candidates, my eye immediately falls on Agnese, a middle-aged robust woman; I ask to speak to her in private. I tell her what her tasks will be and the remuneration if she accepts the job; Agnese observes me pensively and seems a bit hesitant as to whether to accept or not. I think I guess the reasons for her reluctance. I look her in the eyes and say: *I don't want anything sexual from you, I'm in love with a woman who's no longer here, but she's always inside me. You just have to do your work, be the custodian of this house; you'll give the orders for me. These are the keys; you can come and go whenever you want.* Agnese looks me in the eye, nods and says: *I accept.*

From that moment on, at least in Mocomero, life seems to flow normally. I ask Agnese if the market in Lugagnano is still on Friday, she replies affirmatively, warning me: *You can only go there with an armed escort, you have to put your money in your front pockets and never show all your money when you pay...*

The following Friday I go to Lugagnano with Hadas and another guard; we are dressed so as not to attract attention, no rings or watches. As per instructions, I divide the small notes in my pockets. The market is a huge mess; I wait for half an hour for a free parking space, and then walk through the stalls to see if there's anything of interest. I feel observed but not directly threatened. The merchandise on display is mostly cheap and comes from various Asian countries. My eyes fall on some extremely shady characters and I often notice the not too hidden exchange of money for bags of various pills. Suddenly, in the crowd I see my cousin Arcangelo. Our eyes meet, and we look at each other for a few minutes. He's not changed much, in spite of the years; he's just a bit balder and has filled out.

In the corner of my eye I see that he's with three youngsters that I don't like the look of. Hadas puts a hand in his jacket pocket; almost certainly he has his hand on the blaster. The other guard has apparently disappeared, but after a few minutes I realise he's behind Arcangelo and his friends.

We exchange news and so I find out that his father, mother and sister all passed away some time ago; he promises me he'll come to see me in Mocomero, then he'll tell me a lot more; Hadas doesn't look particularly happy, but doesn't say a word and nor do my cousin's friends.

We say goodbye without much warmth. When Arcangelo has gone, I ask Hadas if it's possible to inquire about my relatives' family, he tells me: *You just have to pay and wait.*

Valeria Maria

I've had enough of the market and I get head back to the car, to the the guards' great relief. In the square, as I approach the carpark, I hear a female saying mockingly: *And so you would be, cousin Arturo...* I turn round to look for the woman who says she's my cousin. At first, I can't identify anyone in the crowd, then suddenly my eyes meet those of a young adult. She must be about seventeen, with long curly brown hair; her eyes are bright and deep, she certainly is a beautiful girl but with an arrogant and dissenting look that doesn't suit her.

I ask her: *And who might you be?* Promptly and boldly she answers: *Valeria Maria.* I continue to look at her questioningly and she explains arrogantly who her parents are. She's actually a second cousin, and regardless of her mocking attitude, I like her. I ask: *What can I do for you?* This time she is also ready with her answer: *First of all, you can start by finding me a job so I can get out of this shitty place...* I reply: *Okay, and what would you like to do?*
I like travelling, I guess air steward would be the best bet, but anything would be okay as long as it gets me out of this place, I'm amazed, *air steward? Just that, nothing a bit more specialised?* She looks at me and defiantly as usual says: *What d'you mean? I'm eighteen years old, I speak English, French and Spanish, if you want, you'll find a solution.* I reply laconically: *Yes, anything as long as it doesn't involve studying, from what I can see.* Her eyes flash and she retorts angrily: *I know how to cook and I mean really well... Mr. God Almighty.* She turns and walks off.

Back in Mocomero I make a video call to Katrin in Bergamo and tell her about this meeting and the absurd request of Valeria Maria to find a job as an air steward. Katrin agrees a job as a cook would certainly be easier, but she has contacts with the president of a cooperative aviation service and she'll see what she can do; she also tells me that she'll soon have to return to Israel for her compulsory military retraining. I'll not be able to communicate with her, but I can call her colleague Malka, which in Hebrew means 'Queen' and in one way or another she'll be able to help me.

A few days later, Hadas informs me that my cousin Arcangelo would like to see me. I don't know what he wants, he'll surely want something, he hasn't come here to tell me the story of how the *Diga* (dam) was built or about his family... Hadas is puzzled, he doesn't like the people who were with him in Lugagnano and I think: *I don't either. Alright! Tell him he can come tomorrow at ten.*
The following morning, a few minutes after ten o'clock the bell rings; it's Arcangelo with his three inseparable friends; they don't come in, they say they'll stay outside to smoke. They don't know that Hadas' men are already positioned, unseen, in such a way as to keep an eye on them.

Arcangelo sits down and we look at each other nervously; he doesn't know where to start and I don't know what to say. Agnese prepares coffee and Arcangelo starts by asking me if I remember the good old times and says sadly that unfortunately today things have changed, and for the worse. His tragedy began when his mother Maria was infected by a particular HIV strain. The tests finally showed that his father had infected her and that he got it from a prostitute nicknamed *Bortolona*, whose real name he didn't remember. Some relatives and friends were doing the paperwork to create a charity dedicated to his mother. While he 's talking, I think: *I'm sorry and sad for my aunt, she surely didn't deserve to die that horrible way, however at least this time they can't blame me.*
I ask for news of his sister. Arcangelo's face darkens as he tells me in a bitter voice that unfortunately she was found dead, killed, it's not clear who was responsible. After saying that, he thanks me for the coffee and for my patience in listening to him: *Surely, now that you're back, we'll see each other again.* After he left, I think *Is it possible that this was really just a family visit?* I express my doubts to Hadas, who informs me about Arcangelo's friends' behaviour who stayed outside walking back and forth, smoking, but certainly taking note of different features of the houses and of the various access points. He would task his informant with getting reliable news about Arcangelo and he would increase security at night.

I retire to the House of the Stars and continue to write the book on Francesca, perhaps our story will not interest anyone, but I want her life to be honoured as best it can and to leave a permanent record of her existence. I had started writing this in the hospital, immediately after the terrible event, then here and there, in the moments when I miss her the most. Agnese climbs the steps with the videophone in her hand: *It's Katrin and it's urgent.*

Katrin informs me that one of the air stewards for the night flight from Latam to Rio de Janeiro is ill and they need a temporary replacement: if Valeria Maria can be at Malpensa before 5.00 p.m. she can give it a try, even if it is only a one-off. I call Valeria Maria, when she hears the news, she gawks at me via the monitor: *I'll be there for sure... yes, yes, I have my passport.*

When I manage to get her to listen to me, I take advantage of the moment to give her some instructions: *I'm sending you Hadas with the quantum communicator and some money, in case you need them. You must promise never to go anywhere without the communicator and not go out alone in the streets of Rio. At night time go to the hotel to sleep... You mustn't go out at night... you get it?*

She replies affirmatively: *Whatever you want... thank you.*

Well, I think: *A thank you from Valeria Maria, considering her rebellious nature, that's a great acknowledgment.*

I video call aunt Effa in Buenos Aires, she's an extraordinary woman and is among the people who have been closest to me during my long months in hospital. Effa is happy, she will fly from Buenos Aires to Rio with her mother to meet Valeria Maria, even if only for a couple of hours; she has never met her...

I watch the clock continuously; the quantum communicator gives me the position of Valeria Maria in real time. I see when she takes off, and only then do I go to sleep, the flight takes more than ten hours. In the morning I don't move from the monitors, I see the landing, the airport exit and the bus that brings the crew to the hotel. The hotel is in the suburbs. I hope Valeria Maria is not so foolish as to go out alone. She goes out with a friend by taxi and they are happily taken downtown. Hadas realises how nervous I am and tries to reassure me: *She's with a friend; it's the middle of the day and in the centre... Rio, like all big cities is dangerous and in four hours Effa will arrive, I wonder when she will find the time to rest...* Hadas replies, amused: *She will sleep when she comes home...* I look at him surprised; he's usually indifferent to everything... I see the meeting between Effa, elegant in her black dress, her mother and Valeria Maria, I virtually participate in their embrace.

I keep an eye on the tea room and I control the customers one by one. Two boys immediately notice Valeria Maria and make an advance; she refuses amused, perhaps even thinking that I'm keeping watch on her. Effa and her mother leave for the airport.
Valeria Maria, this time alone, returns to the hotel to prepare for her return.
I notice a suspicious car in front of the hotel, the two boys who were at the tea room get out. When they enter the hotel with a group of tourists, I quickly call the police in Rio: exactly three minutes later a patrol storms into the hall with guns blazing. After about ten minutes the policemen go out with the two men in handcuffs.
I immediately proceed to transfer the 10,000 euros I promised for an emergency. Later I find out that these two boys were stalking pretty girls, drugging them and forcing them into prostitution. With the money I paid, they would surely not be able to do any more damage for a few years. The return trip runs smoothly, the managers of Latam and the cooperative are satisfied with Valeria Maria's work, but it's obvious she doesn't have the skills to do the job permanently.

A few days later, Valeria Maria video calls me, but hasn't lost much of her pride: *Look, you've done nothing but your duty... and it'll be better if you can find me a permanent job... since I can't be an air steward... try as a chef...*
Hadas hears everything and, amused, goes into the next room, while I say in a low voice: *Maybe I shouldn't let her know that for her to earn 5,000 euros, I spent 10,000...*
Early in the evening I tell Katrin everything, she informs me that the following month there's a competition during the *Burtleina* Festival at the Halls Foundation. The contestants have to take part in a cookery contest that will take place in Bergamo in a fortnight. The winner gets to cook for the Festival final evening. The next day I inform Valeria Maria: the competitors have to prepare two dishes typical of Piacenza cuisine, *anolini* (small stuffed pasta) and the

burtleina (type of pancake) as well as the *casoncelli* (stuffed pasta) from Bergamo. She says eagerly: *Sign me up, I've already won!* I think to myself: *Well, if she's half as good a chef as she says she is, and if Katrin has a hand in the competition, then yes, she definitely will win.*

Castelletto and its surroundings

I decide to visit Castelletto, Vezzolacca and then Bardi to see how the places of my youth have changed. Hadas accompanies me with two guards, '*for my safety*'. *The valley reverted to a wilderness, and its inhabitants are as fierce as they once were with strangers. No one with any sense ventures into those places after sunset.*

Memories begin to come back to me as soon as we reach the Dam. At the junction of Morfasso and Castelletto, which we called *Bratel* or harness in the local dialect, my emotions intensified.

The countryside has not changed much, I know that now many houses have bars on the windows and holes here and there in the walls, indicating how people live.

I visit the cemetery where my parents lie, meanwhile my oldest relatives are dust in the churchyard in front of the Old Church.

To Levori: I search in vain for the house where I was born, the fireplace that warmed me; while my thoughts were chasing the flames, a blond angel came to caress my hair. The room where Francesca and I made love until we were exhausted. And my mother, standing between the climbing rose and the door; my grandfather Angelo's smile before his death, the first time I used a shotgun; the swing under the front porch; and the last snow that melts on the outside staircase wall in March.

Unforgettable moments in life. I look towards the valley of *Moja*, towards *Arbarino* and Vezzolacca, I imagine I can see Elvira still dressed in black with her wicker basket, feeling the rustle of the wind in the grass, the smell and the song of the stream, the drops of rain on my face and the sound of chestnuts on the leaves as they fall to the ground... my cheeks are really wet and this time... it's not rain.

The fountain at Bravi is still there, the signs of the time are clearly visible, but the water is still flowing and I stop the car to drink; I hold my hands cupped for a long time under the small trickle of water, incredibly cold, and I slowly taste its coolness in my mouth and throat.

Vezzolacca is silent, the streets deserted and also here there are railings on the windows and holes in the walls of the houses. We return to Bravi and then to Bore, Casali and finally Bardi. There are a lot of people around the streets and in the bars on the square; some faces don't look very trustworthy, and the way they look at me is not very reassuring.

Above, the castle darkly dominates the valley: when I visited it with Francesca and we made love in the dungeons, it looked much more romantic and not so gloomy. The sun is slowly setting, I decide to go back home.

In Luneto, I ask Hadas to stop at the restaurant, he's not very happy, but sends a guard ahead and after a couple of minutes we enter. It is smoky and badly lit with LED lamps, at the bar there are two customers and four or five tables are already busy. I choose a secluded corner, next to a post, not too far from the exit. The choice of location has Hadas' silent approval. Our two guards are sitting at a table not far away, but to cover the side if necessary. The waitress does her best to look friendly and takes orders unenthusiastically. Slowly the place fills up and the customers's voices become a constant singsong. Suddenly a voice I recognise draws me to the next table, half-hidden by the post: it's Gino from Mocomero, it's strange that he's gone out for dinner, especially to Luneto. I lean out slightly and, unseen, I check out the person he's with, it's his nephew Antonio. I didn't see them coming in. They're talking about me, I stop eating and listen, I see that even Hadas has noticed our neighbours' topic of conversation.

Gino: *The Count of Forlanini, bullshit, where does that title come from?* Antonio: *I have known Arturo since childhood, we grew up together and at that time there was no nonsense about any titles. I remember however that my father once talked about someone from his family related to the Count of Forlanini, it seems that he was in submarines during the First World War.*

Gino: *I don't understand why Dr Abele wants to speak to us, and why he made the appointment here rather than Mocomero.*

Antonio: *Probably he didn't want to be noticed by Arturo's men. He must be out of his mind, he never leaves the house. Look, here's the doctor now.*

I'm puzzled, what's Abele doing here? He was my doctor and also for my wife's family, I considered him a great friend. Abele sits down and starts talking, I can't hear everything, but his meaning is clear. He wants to help my ex-wife, according to him she's a very good person. For him, I'm ungrateful and unreliable, he's looking for information on my properties to make me pay what is due my wife.

I've heard enough, I finish eating and taking advantage of a moment when everyone's attention is on a table at the other end where someone screams, I get up, and head quickly to the exit; I pay the owner at the cash desk and I go out without looking back. Hadas and the two guards follow me a few minutes later. I reflect on what I've heard, and reach the conclusion that the situation with my wife must be settled soon. Regardless of my choices and how it ended up for me after hospital and the separation, I still have a great affection for Gina, and I would like her to have a peaceful life.
I realise that I have to find a permanent solution. The day after, I call my publisher. We agree to a simple arrangement, one hundred thousand euros for the rights, sixty thousand to go to my ex-wife and the rest, after expenses, to me. So, I talk to the law firm in Lecco that looks after Gina's interests and fix a meeting with my lawyer to sign the legal documents. Two days later, I go to Lecco with Hadas, sign the documents then return to Mocomero.

The Lugagnano mafia

Hadas, without making too much of it, gives me the report on my cousin, a memory stick including movies and pictures. I retire to the House of Stars and begin to read, I watch all the movies until the end. I'm shaken, unfortunately the reality is worse than I'd imagined. Arcangelo is rotten to the core, and what's more; his buddies are worse than him: drugs, gambling, prostitution, theft, robbery, there's everything and more, and as if this wasn't enough... he's almost certainly the main person behind his sister's murder.

The report explains that there was a lot of friction between the brothers. Like his mother, Arcangelo had never accepted his sister's marriage and, finally, there was major disagreement about their inheritance share.

Hadas asks me: *What do you want to do?*

I say: *They'll arrive, sooner or later, they'll arrive, I'm sure, we should prepare for them.* Hadas replies: *I agree.*

Days pass and life in Mocomero continues normally but there's an intangible tension in the air. I write for a long time in the House of Stars, I read and correct what I'd already written before going to sleep. Francesca is my first and last thought every day.

That evening, before falling asleep, I re-read some old poems, written for Francesca many years before and one in particular takes me back in time.

The silence of the soul

I am waiting for the dawn,
trying to stop the tireless travelling clouds.
I await the hours in distant worlds,
burning thoughts by candlelight,
losing myself in an unknown soul
desperately looking for answers
in other horizons.

Closed in silence

looking for a voice
showing a direction
and time.

I look for memories
faded and foggy,
in the soft nothing
and finally,
in the silence,
I slow down and become nothing.

It's about two o'clock in the morning and Hadas wakes me up abruptly: *They are here.* I get dressed quickly; from the street come the snaps and whistles of the blasters, from the sound I understand they aren't in the stunning position. Hadas has a blaster in each hand; as soon as I touch mine it lights up, I move the selector to kill. Hadas approves and indicates that I should move to the corner where I'll be hidden by the wardrobe and remain stock still; he stays next to me and activates a quantum window. From what I know, anyone getting into the room now will only see an empty space: we're there but we're protected from view by a sort of time bubble. Suddenly the silence returns, from outside and from below, the hisses of weapons can no longer be heard. My skin is crawling when the door slowly begins to open, on the other side there's a shadow, it's not one of my men, and it definitely wears a night visor. An imperceptible beam of light appears from the shadow, and then alights on us; I realise that the light has pierced the quantum screen; Hadas swears in Hebrew: *Benzona* and shields me with his body, taking in the back the shot intended for me. I instinctively pull the trigger towards the shadow which collapses to the ground with a gasp; Hadas is also on the ground. I'm furious, adrenaline is blinding me; I move quickly, I know my house well and I don't need any visor to move in the dark.

I stand on the steps to the study and from there I fire down the stairs, I fire continuously, with each shot the weapon cools a little bit more, until my hand is frozen.

The ghostly darkness is suddenly pierced by the light of my guards' visors who were positioned outside and now enter; I shout: *I'm here,* and the lights are on again. The damage is quite heavy, in addition to Hadas, four of ours are dead, twelve attackers have been hit but... Arcangelo isn't among them. I ask the guards about him and one of them waves his hand to show that he's gone; climbing onto the saddle of one of the attackers' motor bikes I chase him in the direction of Lugagnano.

The road is dark but after the cement works it's straight, I rev up to over 200 kilometres an hour, and, in a few seconds, I'm at the Lugagnano roundabout; has he gone straight to the village? I don't think so: on the bridge there are cameras, for what that's worth, he'll surely choose a secondary road. Then I head on to the ring-road and there I see the lights of what is definitely his car. I approach quickly, and I repeatedly fire at his tyres. Arcangelo evidently didn't expect anyone to follow him; the car begins to slide, goes off the road and rolls over. I stop the bike and I head with my weapon drawn towards the upside-down car. Arcangelo is trying to get out of the broken window, he has a trickle of blood coming from his mouth, I direct the communicator light beam on his face and ask without emotion: *Why?* He sighs deeply and then says: *I was in their debt and they would've killed me if I hadn't.* In return, I ask: *Why didn't you ask me for help when you came to visit me?*
I wanted to but I reckoned my debt was too big and you couldn't have done much.
Why your sister? Arcangelo looks at me angrily, challengingly, and exclaims: *Fuck you!*
Dispassionately, I automatically raise my hand and I pull the trigger; his head explodes. A huge sense of emptiness floods over me, I sit at the edge of the road and I wait for the guards to reach me.

I return to Mocomero in a very sad state and I go to my room; the bodies of Hadas and the aggressor still lie where they fell. From the aggressor's left hand, I remove a black cylindrical device with which he could see inside the quantum bubble.
I'm still thinking about what happened when Katrin, more furious that I've ever seen her, enters the room angrily. She approaches Hadas and, crying, draws signs on his body. My eyes are wide open,

but I'm not sure what I'm seeing: a strange ectoplasmic form comes squawking out of his body, stumbles towards the darkest corner of the room and quickly climbs to the studio ceiling. I believe I see other similar forms, perhaps of the other guards killed; a few seconds later the figures are so well camouflaged in the ceiling beams and the traverses that they disappear from sight.

Meanwhile, Katrin, in a low voice is saying a prayer that I don't understand and then she says: *Rest in peace, Hadas. Thank you, my faithful friend, your incubation will last over a hundred years and then a new Hadas will be reborn and maybe we'll meet again, without knowing.*

Katrin returns, she speaks to me in a very irritated way, she blames me for Hadas dying. I try to explain how things went and how I executed the killer and my cousin with my own hands; she angrily exclaims: *What do I care about them, they are small fish that we could take at any time: but now, I've lost a good friend and a trusted colleague.*

I'm trying to explain that the intruder had managed to see us in the quantum bubble. Katrin looks at me in disbelief, then I show her the instrument found in the aggressor's hand; she grabs it, opens it and carefully looks at the circuits. At that point her voice softens: *It's a Korean device, primitive compared to ours, but effective; sooner or later they would've been introduced here, but I didn't think such technology was already being used by the mafia.*

Her irritation has partly disappeared and I tell Katrin that I too am very saddened for Hadas, I owe him my life and I'd become very attached to him.

Calvary

Katrin tells me: *I have to return to Israel for my military service, I don't know how long for; I won't be able to tell you where I am and communication with the outside is difficult. Malka is like a sister to me, contact her if necessary, she'll find a way to communicate with me. Hadas' place will be taken by Nechama (his name means 'comfort') but you can call him Neche and by Devora (bee, poetess or judge): they will be your shadows; like Hadas; if necessary they will die for you, but I beg you, don't ever sacrifice a life, be cautious. The Lugagnano mafia will not forgive Arcangelo and his acolytes' murders, but if you don't provoke them in their territory, they won't come looking for you.*

I look Katrin deep in the eyes: *What about Valeria Maria, what should I do?* She smiles kindly saying: *Do you like that girl?* I reply: *She's one of the few left in my family, she's a bit like the daughter I never had; yes, even though I'd prefer her to be a little less rude...I like her.*

Katrin looks at me beguilingly and says; *Look, you really don't understand women; anyway she's signed up for the competition and she should have a job for a while; then Malka will help you find her a job.*

Thanks, Katrin! Thanks for everything you do for me, sometimes I wonder why you do it, you know too well that I can't repay all this.

Katrin replies: *We should all do what we're able to do. D'you remember the zen fable of the scorpion? Well... one good turn deserves another, to anyone who needs it, without a reason... in this way you'll repay your debt to me...*

Katrin is gone. Now, once a week, I call Malka; I know she keeps an eye on me through a quantum window and that Neche and Devora inform her regularly. I don't know any more about Katrin even though I ask about her all the time.

The day for the competition arrives, Valeria Maria leaves for Bergamo and Malka takes care of her; I'm calm, she's not taking risks where she's going, and she's in good hands. The competition lasts all day Saturday and the results will be annnounced on Sunday in the late afternoon. The day after, at 4.55 p.m. I tune the monitors to

Bergamo News and finally hear: the competition was won by Valeria Maria, Sonia Conte in second place and Lina Campo in third... all three from Piacenza. I have some lingering doubts: *Are they really so good or... did Katrin fix it before leaving?* This I will never know for sure. Monday morning Valeria Maria video calls me, she is radiant and excited, she has two weeks to produce the mandatory medical certificate to cook for the public, and it's done; she doesn't thank me and, even if this doesn't surprise me much, I did expect at least a thank you from her.

A week later it's a completely different, Valeria Maria's at the videophone early in the morning: she looks shocked, pained, with dark circles under her eyes and a sad look: *I'm infected, I'm infected, d'you understand? Please, I have only you, don't leave me.*
She starts sobbing, in my heart I hope it's not what I imagine, I say: *Calm down, Valeria Maria, calm down; we'll find a solution, I'll send Devora to get you.*
An hour later Valeria Maria arrives at Mocomero, comes in and hugs me, holding me tightly, sobbing desperately. I'm surprised by that embrace, I realise after all Valeria Maria is a girl attempting to look like a woman but... is not yet a woman. She says that she didn't pay too much attention to the doctor when she took the stick with the results... she just signed with her fingerprint then returned home. When she looked at the results and had taken them in, she felt like dying and cried all night, then at dawn she called me. I take the stick, connect it to the computer and start reading page after page. Sex, age, height, weight, race, build, virgin, blood type, DNA and blood analysis: and here's the problem... she's infected with the HIV2 CRF-884 strain. The doctor who signed off the test results suggests: *Immediate admission to a specialist facility.* As the detected infection is contagious, this has been automatically reported to the relevant authorities.

I check the internet about the CRF-884 strain and what I read scares me; it's much more dangerous than the one I caught, if not treated you get ill in just over a year. Fortunately, over time medicine has made giant strides and I'll leave no stone unturned for Valeria Maria.

I stop looking at the monitor and look her straight in the eyes: *Valeria Maria, but here it says you're a virgin, how did you catch the virus?* She looks down and doesn't answer, I insist: *Please, I want to help you, trust me and tell me how it happened.*

Valeria Maria looks up angrily and unbuttons her blouse, undoes her bra and defiantly shows me her naked breasts. At first, I don't understand, they look like normal breasts, then I put on my glasses and see better, around the nipples and areolas there are scars, now healing; I observe more clearly... it's not possible, they look like teeth, as if someone has bitten her breasts.

I look at her and again, I don't understand, Valeria Maria gets dressed and begins to tell her story. *When my mother died, my father was God knows where, and I was hungry, no one would give me a job, but I didn't want to become a whore... Arcangelo suggested I have hormone injections to encourage milk production. His friends at the club were willing to pay a lot of money to drink 'virgin milk at the source'; more than one bit me fiercely and that's how I was infected by someone whose gums were bleeding.*

Valeria Maria, still without looking me in the eye continues: *Our dear cousin also wanted to sell my virginity for a very high price so he could half his debts; however, I met you in Lugagnano and I asked for your help... at that point Arcangelo understood that I'd escaped his control and with his friends he tried to get rid of you...*

I get up to avoid being sick and walk back and forth. My mother used to say that life could be very dirty; she's right, but it's the men who make it dirty. Devora is impassive in a corner. After a few minutes I ask Valeria Maria: *Why didn't you tell me everything before, you behaved so arrogantly?*

Now Valeria Maria looks at me pleading: *Forgive me if I didn't warn you, I was desperate and I was afraid that you would say no, I wanted to be sure to get your attention.* Even if the situation's tragic, a slight smile lingers over my face and I say to myself: *If that's what you wanted, you did it, you definitely did it.*

Valeria Maria looks at me and continues with a trembling voice: *If you leave me homeless I'm finished; I need you. Will you help me?*

I reply: *Yes, Valeria Maria, I'll do everything possible, tomorrow I'll call Malka and I'll try to inform Dr. Katrin Or who cured me; while you're here, I'll stay in the guest room and you can sleep in my room.*

138

Valeria Maria says: *No, please, I'll sleep in the guest room, I'd feel embarrassed sleeping in Francesca's bed.* I'm too surprised to get angry: *How do you know about Francesca...?*

Valeria Maria doesn't answer and, together with Devora, she goes up to her room; I look at Agnese and she acts as if nothing's happened. I send the medical notes to Malka, I hope she can arrange hospitalisation as soon as possible, I also ask her to send them to Katrin in Israel.

Early in the morning, I video call Malka and I ask her to contact Katrin Or: I trust only her to do the therapy. Malka tries to dissuade me, the Foundation doctors know how to treat these cases and she asks me to bring Valeria Maria as soon as possible to Bergamo. She'll undergo treatment with radiation that, little by little, together with the correct drugs, will reduce the presence of the virus in her blood and in her DNA until they get rid of it. It is more or less the same treatment carried out on me and will last between six and nine months. However, today the therapy and the machines are much more advanced and the success rate is over 70%. I insist, *Seventy percent is not enough for me, I want one hundred percent.* While I speak, I do not realise Valeria Maria has entered the House of Stars in her nightgown and has listened in silence to the whole conversation; when I turn off the monitor I feel her presence, but I don't have time to get up, she hugs me from behind, gives me a kiss on the head and whispers: *Thank you.*

After breakfast we inform the Halls Foundation, aware that the prizes will now be awarded to the next three women in the competition. I know Sonia well, I was at her wedding and I know that she now lives on the other side of the Arda river in Vicanino. She runs a farm with chickens, rabbits and cows. If Sonia learnt from her foster mother, then she is definitely a good cook. I also know Lina, she was a childhood friend of mine in *Molinello* and I think she's a good cook too. I don't know the fourth woman. Bad luck for this missed opportunity, but Valeria Maria's life is worth much more.

I warn Valeria Maria to be ready as soon as Malka calls us to leave for Bergamo; she moves her head in denial: *I'll go with Devora, it's pointless for you to come with me; today there'll only be the usual paperwork and they'll repeat the tests. I would prefer you to come and see me in a few days... really, I'll need you then.*

The moment arrives for Valeria Maria to leave Mocomero; she goes out without turning round, maybe so as not to cry or... not to make me feel bad. I have a bad feeling that she will never come back to Mocomero and, if she does, it will almost certainly not be with me. I advise Malka and I urge her to send the medical records to Doctor Or and, once it's prepared, the treatment plan.

A week later I go with Neche to Bergamo. It makes a strange impression on me to return to those hospital wards, it looks completely different from when I was hospitalised there. I have to wear a sterile suit, hat, mask and gloves, this is the only way I can enter the department where they're taking care of Valeria Maria. A nurse accompanies me to the section where the flow machines operate: little by little, they are neutralising the virus in her blood and DNA. Valeria Maria is standing, in panties and bra, leaning, slightly bent over on a machine that looks made of crystal and from which light blue streams are emitted, appearing to travel through her whole body.

Valeria Maria perceives my presence and turns her head slightly; she recognises me and smiles saying *Hey! Hi, sorry for this ridiculous position, I've got to stay like this for another two hours today.*
How are you, Valeria Maria? Her voice is serious, this time: *I'm doing my best, I want to get out of here as soon as possible, it's really boring.* I look at her and say seriously: *Okay, you have to get better so you can live your life with dignity.* She asks me: *How long it will take, in your opinion? Here they're very vague about it.*
I reply: *Six months if everything goes well, but say eight: if it's over before, you'll feel like a lioness, but if you think six and then it takes eight, you'll go into depression.* Valeria Maria blurts out in Spanish: *La puta que lo parió... ochos meses de mierda,* (what a bitch, eight months of this shit) and then asks me: *What will you do now?* I think, 'What am I going to do?' Then I ask myself mentally, what would Francesca do, she was as stubborn as a mule and as brave

140

as a tiger, she would have left no stone unturned, she would have knocked on all the doors, just as she did that time she risked losing her home.

I answer: *I think I'll go to Israel, I have to talk to Katrin Or. I'm sure they're very good here, but I only trust her.*

The nurse tells me the time for the visit is over, I can't hug Valeria Maria, but I promise I'll be back soon to visit her.

I leave the wards with Neche and head, not far, to Malka's office.

I inform her I've decided to go to Israel; she observes me without speaking and then she says: *Alright, but I'm not sure when Katrin will be able to see you and where. I'll inform her where you are in Israel and she'll contact you to tell you where you can meet.*

Israel

I return to Mocomero and I look for a convenient flight to Tel Aviv: there is a direct one every Friday from Parma, but there are no seats available. Francesca would not give up, so I phone the airline: they tentatively accept my reservation; I am on stand-by. On Thursday afternoon they inform me there's a spare seat. None of the procedures have changed, there is the usual security questioning by Israeli soldiers. In any case, the Israelis already know everything about me; they have my photos, fingerprints and images of my retina. I answer the girl's questions: *Who prepared your suitcase? How did you get to the airport? Have you ever lost sight of your luggage? Has anyone given you a package to take to Israel? This is for your safety — can you check that everything in your baggage is yours? Why are you going to Israel? Is it the first time...?* I answer this last question: *No, this must be the tenth or eleventh time.*

Excuse me for a moment, and she goes away, talks with a small group, and another guard comes back to me with my passport in his hand... he starts again with the same questions, then urges: *Have you ever been to Jerusalem and the occupied territories?* I answer: *Almost every time with my guide, Ester Arditti,* he replies: *Arditti? Never heard of her, I don't know her.* I calmly say: *You should! She was the only Israeli woman to have been awarded a gold medal for both civil and military honour.* Finally, the guard says: *Sorry for the double check,* and he hands me the passport with a formal *Shalom.*

While I'm closing the bag, an apparently harmless old man, who was watching everything from afar, passes close to me and murmurs in English, in a low voice: *These young people, they don't know their history!* I look at him and smile serenely.

The plane is full of religious tourists visiting the holy land; I immediately recognise the Israeli service man, sitting indifferently at the back of the plane. The flight takes just over three hours, and everything goes well until someone has the bright idea of saying the rosary.

Upon arrival, I am among the first to get through passport control, leaving the horde of pilgrims behind; I go out and rent a small

Japanese car with air conditioning. I don't need a big car. I head to Netanya to what was once the Park Hotel, and book in. The hotel is one of the few providing a clean room for sixty dollars a day; breakfast is nothing special, but for that price...

To get to Netanya I have to drive through the whole of Tel Aviv, the seaside town is directly on the opposite side to the Ben Gurion airport. I pass the sign for the Dan Hotel, then that of the Carlton, then to the right to Dizengoff square, and finally the Sheraton. On the right there used to be a restaurant, The little Tel Aviv but it's no longer there; everything has been concentrated into shopping centres like in the United States.

Once in the hotel I get in touch with Itzik, one of my few friends still active, even if retired: he promises me that we'll meet for dinner one evening and he'll bring Giora too. He'll pick him up, because his colleague doesn't drive any more. I don't want to disturb Micha Danziger or Chanoki, I'll phone them before leaving and I'll do the same with Eliah Spiegel.

From my fifth floor window, I can see a corner of the sea; on the balcony walls, exactly as in the past, blunt needles, attached by silicon, prevent pigeons from landing. Today is the Sabbath: not even the lift or the toaster will work until sunset. It's early in the morning and I go alone down to the sea. I sit on a bench and wait for the sunrise, I look at the sea, and I remember that same place and the same sea, in another time, on the other side, in Giardini Naxos. Francesca jumped out of bed in her pyjamas and ran towards the window, she wanted to see the sun rise on the sea, I hugged her from behind and we waited together. Now I am aware that this was one of the tenderest moments of my life with her.

Lost as I was in my memories, I had not realised that the sun was now high in the sky. I get up and go to a central bar for a decent coffee.

I spend the morning writing, between one coffee and another, there aren't many tourists at this time of year and the bartender isn't in a hurry to send me away. I look for a small restaurant, pitta and hummus with some fruit are enough for today, I don't plan to drive,

143

and I indulge in a Maccabee beer. I walk through Netanya and then go back to the hotel to rest. In the evening dinner with Itzik and Giora has been arranged in a seaside restaurant not far away. I have a Mantero scarf for each of their wives. Seeing old friends warms my heart, we exchange relevant news, some memories and finally a shalom shalom late at night.

I have to ring the hotel bell to have the front door opened; I ask for a bottle of water and I go to bed.

It's Sunday, I have no intention of spending my day in the confusion of Tel Aviv, I go to Caesarea and Haifa to see the Bahai gardens, then to Galilee up to Tiberias and back. I won't call Michael, I's like to see him but I think he's too old now to leave his house. Katrin can track me through the videophone or the quantum viewer. My day passes calmly; I stop in places that attract my attention, even if they're not strictly touristic. A light lunch in a small restaurant, pitta, hummus and mineral water, I also try some beautiful Caesarea strawberries. I've already visited these places many times for both leisure and work, but there's always something new to see. I get back late in the evening. For dinner, I make do with a few dates I bought in the market. The next day, Monday, I plan to visit Jerusalem, I could get there today via the Jericho detour, but the Holy City deserves at least a day.

I leave Netanya around nine in the morning, the Tel Aviv traffic rush hour is over; I arrive in sight of Jerusalem at eleven. I park near the Dung Gate, from where I walk to the old city. A quick glance at the Western wall, then through the check point I get to the Arab part of the city. Today I don't want to be consumed by memories; I want to mix with people: someone once said that *People are the biggest show in the world and it's for free.* The mixture of races, cultures and religions in Jerusalem is unique and in that human chaos everyone seeks their own path. Of course, most are pilgrims from all over the world, confounding sounds and colours moving towards the Holy Sepulchre. I stop for a moment, yes, this should be the side street with the Arab restaurant I'm looking for and here it is. The tables are set in a marble-walled room and it's cool even though the sun is hot. The kitchen is across the street. The waiter looks at me surprised, since I enter as if I know the place well; then the owner arrives with the menu and observes me carefully, probably I remind him of someone. At that point I say: *I knew your father, I came here often with Ester Arditti.* His face lights up: *Now I remember.* I don't look at the menu, I ask for: *Lamb ribs, pitta, hummus and sparkling water.* He smiles: *Only a few minutes, sir.* He certainly chooses the best ribs because they are the tastiest I've ever eaten.

I ask for the bill and leave a generous tip.

At last I get a message on the videophone from Malka: *Tomorrow, go to the Arava, on the spice route, stay at the B & B near Hatseba, between the Dead Sea and the Red Sea, Katrin will contact you there.* I'd been to the Arava a long time ago, it's right at the bottom end of Israel, it's about 350 km, which means four hours by car. I have to go to bed early, I walk a little bit in Jerusalem, then I go to the exit for the Jewish side, there are fewer people and I can walk more quickly. The steering wheel of the car is hot, wetting a cloth with mineral water it's cool enough for me to drive.

I give up the hotel room for a couple of nights and on Tuesday, at five in the morning, I leave for Arava. I prefer to travel in the cooler hours, as, even with the air conditioning, it's hot and this way I can also avoid rush hour traffic. I take the road to Ashkelon, then continue to Sderot, leaving the Gaza strip on my right and then straight to Beer Sheva. From there I continue in the direction of Eilat. I arrive at Arava and ask for directions to the Moshav Hatseba, it is not very far. At eleven. they give me a room in a wooden house in the shade of the trees. I lie down on the bed and fall asleep, I wake up after a couple of hours but it's still too hot to go out and visit the Moshav.

At seven I take advantage of the abundant dinner: I eat a lot of fruit, avocado, mango and watermelon; the coffee is far from Italian standards, but the tea is delicious. The quantum locator tells me there's an unread message: *Tomorrow at ten, someone will come and get you. Shalom, K.*

On Wednesday, at ten past ten a light pick-up driven by an

olive-skinned man is waiting for me, the only word he says is: *Shalom*. He drives fast to the centre of Eilat and from there to the peripheral residential area.

The pick-up stops in front of a chalet in a genteel neighbourhood with many trees and very clean streets. Katrin comes to the door, dressed in a light linen shirt and trousers, she hugs me smiling, invites me to sit in a small living room with a coffee table; she pours me coffee and gives me a small dish with a generous portion of cake. After the customary pleasantries, I show her the stick with Valeria Maria's medical records. Katrin connects the stick to her laptop, quickly scrolls through the documents to the treatment plan, and studies it carefully, taking notes from time to time. A good half hour has passed and then she turns off the monitor and asks if she can keep the stick. I answer, *Yes, I have a copy of it in Mocomero.*
Katrin: *I hope you'll have lunch with me, I took a day off, but I have to go back in. I'll cook something very simple.* I reply: *Certainly, what would I do on my own?*

While she's at the stove, Katrin informs me that this was her parents' house, she returns here from time to time and during the holidays. The house is co-owned with her brother, but — for the time being — neither of them wants to sell it. She has a small flat in Tel Aviv where she lives when not abroad. After lunch, during coffee, at some point Katrin says: *Arturo, what I'm about to tell you is confidential and, please, keep it to yourself. Let me inform my superiors and colleagues in the right way at the right time. I know I can trust you.*
I look at her and I nod: *I don't think I'll go back to Europe, they offered me a job and a good salary at the hospital in Tel Aviv; they need me here too. And there's also another reason: I would like to have children before I'm too old to do so.*
I let her words sink in, and then I say: *Katrin I hope you find the right soulmate, as I did, and that you can be happy, as I was. I only hope it's for life... with children you'll have much more, I didn't have children...* then I add: *There is Valeria Maria, however, who for me is like a daughter...*
Katrin: *Yes, I've been thinking about Valeria Maria's situation;*

Malka had already informed me, I think they're applying the correct therapy; I only have some small suggestions in mind that I'll send to my colleagues in Bergamo. The virus strain that's infected her is one of the most dangerous, but it was diagnosed in time, before it could do irreversible damage. The only change I would suggest is that they use a new experimental drug that apparently has fewer side effects, however the treatment time will be unchanged. If she reacts well, which seems to be the case, she'll be able to lead a normal life and have healthy children.

I think for a while then answer: *Thanks, Katrin, you know I owe you a lot.* She snorts: *We've already had this discussion and now what will you do?*

The question slightly surprises me, *I'm thinking about it, I confess that I've no clear ideas, the book's almost finished, it will still take me a couple of months. An English friend, Jeremy, asked me to speak at a conference in Nairobi, maybe I'll go there. I like to share my experiences, now I'm also aware that 'thinking you know is the worst ignorance,' but ultimately I am the result of all my teachers' teachings and it's right to pass on my experience to others... Someone once said: 'The world can only be saved by the breath of education.'*

Katrin reflects and then says: *Why don't you find a woman, you're a mature man who has a certain charm, it shouldn't be difficult, it would change your life, and... Francesca would want it.*

Hearing Francesca's name, I light up and smile: *You're right, Francesca's always been a free woman, independent and rebellious... she would want it... My relationship with her wasn't conventional, we were both free to do what we wanted, there were no obligations, and yet... when I met her, my search was over. Francesca tiptoed into me and gradually occupied my soul... totally. She's still with me, I feel her by my side, she doesn't order me around, she doesn't guide me, she doesn't impose herself... and yet there... I think... I think I'm at one with Francesca. There's something else I feel deep inside, that I know well but I don't want to see right now and it's ... that my life is about to end...*

The time for farewell has come, we hug each other and that hug says it all... I go out without turning back, and the pick-up brings me back to the Moshav. I pay the bill; the next morning I leave early for

Tel Aviv; the day after tomorrow is Friday and my flight to Parma. Irit, the wife of the moshavim, prepares a package with breakfast for my journey, I thank her, and go to bed. Early in the morning, about four I get up and head towards Sodom, I leave the main road, park the car at the bottom of a hill, I walk up and sit down on a rock.

I wait for the sun to rise in the east, in Jordan. I'm in the so-called 'asshole of the world', more than 450 metres below sea level; the silence is total, all around are only rocks and desert. The sun is now high and casts a ghostly light around, I need not hurry to get to Netanya, I have time to visit Masada too. I arrive at the hotel in the evening, I pay the bill and I go to bed. I get up at five, I have to return the car at the airport, and then there's the check-in process. At noon the plane takes off. At Arrivals in Parma airport, Neche is waiting for me and one hour later I'm back in Mocomero.

I call Malka, she confirms she's received Katrin's instructions and organises a visit to Valeria Maria on Sunday. In the hospital, I follow the signposts and I make my way up to the infectious diseases ward. There's the ritual of gowning-up with overalls, gloves and mask and finally they take me to room 34. Valeria Maria lights up when she sees me; I sit down and tell her about my trip to Israel, about my meeting with Katrin, without neglecting anything, except for the fact that she won't be coming back to work in Bergamo.

Valeria Maria listens and finally says: *Well, at least you've travelled, here every day is the same; I don't need to tell you anything more because you know how it is, this life, since you've already lived it... You should find a woman.*

I reply: *I already have one, Valeria Maria, I already have her.* She says passionately: *Don't talk nonsense, Francesca is gone.*

I say: *She's with me, perhaps more than before; if it's true that each of us can be what we say we are, she's me, and I'm her.*

'Comprendere', the Italian verb for 'to understand' comes from the Latin 'cum prendere', that means to become. Valeria Maria, when you read the book I'm writing, maybe you'll understand: I didn't have many women, but I had some, all different. I'm grateful to them, some of them used me, some of them loved me. One, for sure, loved me much more than I loved her, maybe some of them were even indifferent to me, there're also those who hurt me really badly... yet

each of them gave me something, they helped me to grow, to mature. With all those women there was always a part of me that remained indifferent and, after making love, I had to detach myself: I got up and went to smoke. I'm not perfect and neither's Francesca, sometimes she has her problems, she's anxious and has too big a heart, yet she's the right woman for me.

With Francesca, from the first kiss, it's total involvement, without limits or boundaries. Making love is beautiful before, during and after... with her I don't go out after making love, rather it's the moment of the sweetest and deepest tenderness. With Francesca love is every thought, the first when I wake up and the last before falling asleep, when we drink coffee, or go to the seaside, or the mountains or just shopping at the supermarket: love is every moment of life.

Valeria Maria looks at me pensively and then says: *You're crazier than I thought, I understand that you really love Francesca, however I still think you can have another woman, without necessarily loving her so much.*

A nurse arrives. Valeria Maria relaxes on the bed and offers her arm for the antiviral drip. I hold her free hand, and feel her firm grip through the glove; I look her in the eyes and smile... *I'll be back to see you soon.*

Kenya

The book is finished, now I have to send it to my two trusted friends, Claudio, good at editing and correcting grammar and Angelo, a writer and poet and good friend since the seventies. A few years ago, I sent him a booklet of poems I wrote for Francesca, some of them written in Argentina. When I got the manuscript back, I felt demoralised: from over fifty poems he had deleted at least forty. Angelo's comment was severe: *You come over like a young man in the army sending letters to his girlfriend every day, writing 'te vojo ben'* (I love you in Venetian dialect). *Wait a bit, then read it again.* Of course, he was right. However, Angelo was too wise to leave me without hope, and his comments on the few remaining poems raised me sky-high.

The invitation from Jeremy to go to Kenya arrives. I have to decide whether or not to accept, on impulse I say yes, and I book the flight via Paris with Air France. I call Malka and inform her that as far as Mocomero is concerned, I'll only need one unit to control the house from time to time. I say goodbye to Neche and Devora; now they'll return to headquarters with the other guards and maybe they'll be happy that the Count of Forlanini is leaving.

The flight is from Linate to Charles de Gaulle, the airport in the shape of a horseshoe, and boarding for Nairobi is over the other side so you need to take the bus.
Behind me on the plane are two Chinese men, both well-built and smiling; the youngest greets me in English, I answer: *Hi, have a nice flight.* After an hour, to stretch my legs, I walk to the end of the half-empty plane and sit in a seat at the back. After a while, the young Chinese man joins me in a nearby seat. He would like to chat and starts with: *Why are you flying to Nairobi?* I calmly reply for a conference on flowers; he tells me that his boss has sent him and his colleague to Kenya *to buy a hotel.* I'm surprised and ask if he knows where; his answer surprises me: *No, we still have no idea where; we'll only go back to Bejing after we have bought it, it could be in Nairobi, or in Lamù, Malindi or Monbasa, who knows!* He keeps asking me

where I'm from; to make it short, I say Italian, from Milan and he replies: *Oh, I'm often in Milan for trade exhibitions, but it's no good: Italians want me to sell for them and no one wants to buy anything from me.* I reply: *Oh, yes, what do you sell?* As quick as a flash he replies: *Everything! You can ask me for anything from China and I provide it.* He gives me his business card, I give him mine and stay silent. After a few minutes he asks: *How are the women in Kenya?* I answer: *I don't know, it's the first time I've ever been to Kenya.* Actually, I've been to other African countries, but I don't want to dwell on this. The Chinese man doesn't give up and asks: *How much does a woman cost in Kenya?* I answer: *As I told you, I don't know, I've never been there.* He asks again: *How much does it cost in Italy?* Now I'm also amused: *Well, it depends on the class and the length of the service; I'm not very well-informed but I think anything from thirty to four hundred or even a thousand dollars or more, it depends.* This time it's him looking at me in amazement: *In Bejing a...* he makes a sign with his fingers on his mouth to indicate 'exquisite', and then lifting one finger exclaims: '*One dollar!*'

Luckily, we are landing, and everyone has to return to their place.

While I'm queuing for my entry visa, I see Jeremy a little further on; I call him and he joins me. When they check my documents, he asks me if I can lend him a hundred dollars, as he only has pounds with him. As an Englishman he has to pay for a visa, I don't, as I'm Italian. Sometimes being Italian has its advantages.

I have to talk about the state of floriculture in Italy, Europe and the Middle East; I give Jeremy my presentation and I go to bed. Being in Nairobi, the hotel has all the usual comforts, the breakfast buffet is well-stocked, and I make the most of this opportunity, since I didn't have any dinner.

The conference room is in a nearby neighbourhood, the local floriculture exhibition is in the same building. We walk to the seminar in a group. At eleven there's the ceremonial ribbon cutting and the official inauguration. After lunch, there will be technical reports, I will be the third speaker. In the meantime, I talk with several people I've known for a long time, like Hartmut from Germany and David from the United States; I easily make friends with several other technicians. I take the microphone and I describe the situation of floriculture without frills, emphasising the critical issues but also the really big trends. I reply steadily to the questions that I'm asked, until Jeremy, as moderator, invites me to the round table the next day. Of course, I'll be there; I wouldn't have any idea where to go otherwise.

The day after, the Nirp boys arrive from Italy: they are exhibiting their roses at the fair and will join our group for a tour of the companies, then they will also visit their propagators and licensees in Kenya. There's also a French rose-grower, accompanied by a woman of a certain age, but very beautiful and elegant. They tell me that they were on the same plane as me, even if I hadn't noticed them, and that they'd remained shut up in the hotel because of problems caused by the vaccines: I didn't have the shots because they weren't mandatory.

Later I discover the woman's a former model, the rose-grower's lover and here unbeknown to the grower's wife. Lydia, as she's called, speaks Italian well, has a son in Milan and a house in Piedmont. With barely concealed irritation, her boyfriend notices the growing friendship between us, we happily talk for hours.
In the evening we go to a typical restaurant where they serve various types of grilled meat. David, together with a couple of Dutch salesmen, who are sponsoring the dinner, talks for hours. David also speaks Spanish and is a great connoisseur of Colombian and Latin American floriculture, I listen to him with interest, we never stop learning. Lydia is sitting with her boyfriend, Marie Françoise and other people, who I assume are also French. I can't talk to her because I'm too far away but sometimes our eyes meet.

In the hotel as we make for our rooms, Lydia approaches and tells me, nodding toward her boyfriend: *Il est en colère parce qu'il pense que tu veux m'inviter au lit.* (He's angry because he thinks you want to take me to bed.) I smile and with a hint of denial, I reply: *Vous le méritez sûrement, vous êtes une femme charmante mais pour le moment je pense qu'il vaut mieux être amis.* (I'm sure it'd be worth it, you're a charming woman, but I think for the moment it's better to stay just as friends.) Before falling asleep I think about Lydia, surely it could happen, it has already happened with other women in the past, but even though she's an extremely attractive woman, my soul is in turmoil and too distant from her, besides my body doesn't react to hers. Francesca, however, is always with me and accompanies me in sleep and when I'm awake, just as Alda Merini said: *Amore mio ho sognato di te come si sogna della rosa e del vento.* (My love, I dreamed of you as one dreams of rose and the wind.)

In the morning with Jeremy and David, and a farmer of Indian origin at the wheel of a Jeep, we headed towards Lake Naivasha where Sulmac, a well-established company is situated. It had started with the name of DCK in Sardinia, then it became DCK East Africa and finally it was reborn in Kenya as Sulmac. On the road, just outside Nairobi, there's a police checkpoint, but the officer, noticing we're white, lets us pass immediately.

We stop to admire the beauty of the hills and valleys, it is a breath-taking view, on a promontory a group of Masai observes us indifferently. Yes, perhaps this is precisely that Africa that inspired Karen Blixen; I'd have given anything to hold Francesca in my arms and to observe this beauty with her eyes.

We go back to Nairobi after dark, at dinner in the hotel I meet a certain Hamilton from the British company CDC who asks me many questions about floriculture; I reply as best I can, especially on future trends. He explains to me that CDC has a large grant from the British government, but they can only invest in non-EU countries.

The day after, we have more technical visits. In the meantime, we learn that Marie Françoise was attacked and robbed of her necklace and watch on her way back from the exhibition to the hotel. David says nothing, but Jeremy emphasises: *And to think that she's the one out of all of us with the most experience of Nairobi, and it had to happen to her...*

At lunch, Hamilton and I continue to talk about the market, David is strangely silent. I point out David's mood to Jeremy and he, with typical British humour, blurts out: *Maybe he's run out of words.*

I also ask for some more information on Hamilton. Jeremy explains to me that, without meaning to, I've become involved in delicate CDC negotiations to acquire Sulmac.

While I settle my hotel bill, Hamilton offers to take me to the airport in his agency car. I accept willingly. During the journey Hamilton informs me that he'll contact me thorough his secretary, who's of Italian origin, to promote CDC.

While I'm waiting to board, I meet up with Lydia and her boyfriend at the gate. We talk a bit about our trip to Africa, about the randomness of meetings; Lydia looks at me with bright eyes as we exchange business cards. I think Lydia's a woman who's seen it all, and she knows exactly where she's going. She knows men inside out, a lot better than I understand women. She understood very well that my heart was out of reach, but she likes to play and she's been fooling around with me; she's also aware that I know all of this, and then I wonder why she's pretending to flirt? Maybe... maybe she's curious to know and meet the woman who has totally taken possession of my heart.

The plane to Paris is full, I'm sitting quite a way from Lydia and her boyfriend, early in the morning in the confusion of landing I lose sight of them, I have to run as I have little time before my plane for Milan takes off and I have to get to the other side of the airport.

Teaching

Transfer knowledge unchanged: knowledge is not an individual, but a collective asset. This is what I answered to the first question asked by Katrin (I think it was her) in Barcelona. I want to put this belief into practice. I've always liked teaching and have helped many students to graduate, but also ordinary people. It's something I've always done because it's in my nature and not because I earned money from it. From time to time I have met up again with some of these people years later, and I was often surprised to hear some of them saying: *Arturo, you are the person who changed my life.* I don't even remember meeting some of these people, so, when I asked one woman: *In what sense did I change your life?* The answer was: *I was very confused and didn't know what to do. I met you at the exhibition and I asked you for advice, you pointed me to that school and to the studio where I practised; if today I have become the landscape designer that I am, it's down to you.*

Actually, these people have become what they are because they have sweated and worked hard to get where they are, but yes... I like to think that I played a small part.

My book's in print, in only a few weeks the launch will take place, as planned, at the Bergamo Foundation Halls.

I give my courses in Cinisello Balsamo, in the suburbs of Milan, in a grey and gloomy Trade Union building. When I asked the preliminary questions to get to know the students, what their expectations were, and especially what they expected from my lessons, one of them very honestly explained to me that, around Milan, the winters are wet, grey and depressing. Many of the students were there just to stay warm and wait for 5 p.m. to go home. With the excuse of taking the refresher course, they received their salaries just the same, but didn't have to spend the day in the cold and wet.

Hearing this makes me want to walk out of the classroom straightaway. I'm paid twenty-five euros net per hour, and this may be right, but no one's interested in what I have to communicate? I find this very humiliating. Then, in the end, I say to myself, *Alright, but this doesn't mean I shouldn't do my job properly.* I try extra hard to make the lessons interesting, I use anecdotes and facts that really happened, life lessons to be taken as an example. In short, I try to provide the trainees with the basic tools, that is to say, logic and common sense that will allow them to get to the nub of problems that could arise in their lives and help them work out the answers. I try to draw out everyone's abilities and develop them. More than one student asks me for a copy of my book, I give them the diagrams and the notes, the book will be available in a few days. I tell them about my life, I use it as an example and day after day their attention is revived and their ability to reason is refined.

We have reached the end of the course, in the afternoon the organisers will deliver the certificates and have prepared refreshments. Parents, friends and relatives are also present. Amongst them are Anna, my ex-wife's sister and her daughter; they tell me I'm not behaving well, that Gina's still waiting for me and that I'm wrong to be prejudiced against my niece because she's hooked up with a black man.

A middle-aged woman, clearly from southern Italy, also approaches me; she's the mother of one of the most intelligent students on the course and she reproaches me: *You're a bad example for the boys and you shouldn't be teaching; my son's changed, he's not himself anymore since he started attending your lessons. You should understand that your attitude is irresponsible, and it's ruining people.*
I would like to say: *Madam, maybe I'm not a champion of morality, but it's the opposite: I try to teach that knowledge is the basis for responsibility and that we can't take responsibility for something we don't know.* I'm disgusted and I'm about to leave, when the director approaches me and kindly tells me *Arturo, everyone has specifically asked that you give the final greeting, please take the microphone...*

The book launch

I spend Christmas on my own in Mocomero, the house is silent, too silent, I press some buttons on the stereo and the music brings some colour to the surroundings. I move the small nativity scene in its ceramic tray on to the sideboard together with Francesca's miniature Christmas trees. I light the fire in the fireplace, just to bring some life to the place. I think: *I'm not in Castelletto and the blonde queen who strokes your hair is not here either.* I burn a stick of incense and arrange the table for two, saying aloud: Today *anolini...*
On the afternoon of new Year's Eve, I remove the doorbell, close the shutters, make sure that everything's in order and that the lights are off. I lock the door and say to the house: *Goodbye, thank you for looking after me, I hope I will come back one day...*

I am wearing my dark dress YSL suit, the blue shirt with the French collar, a Herman Brood sweater and tie, a gift from Rob Zurel, I also have a dark anorak although I don't plan to wear it. I make for Bergamo on the motorway, I have all the time in the world and I don't need to hurry; I say to myself: *I have been in a rush all of my life.*
First step, visiting Valeria Maria: in a couple of months she'll be discharged. This time I'm allowed in her room without the protective suit; but even if there're no more real risks I have been advised to avoid any physical contact. I find Valeria Maria different, more mature and much more womanly. *Haven't you noticed anything? Look at my hair! The hairdresser has literally just left, I arranged it especially for you.* I smile, *So this is why you look even more beautiful and charming!*
I put a copy of my book on the table. *The dedication, did you write me a dedication?* I take up the book and write quickly on the first page: *To Valeria Maria, always viva la vita forever,* and sign my name.
Valeria Maria opens the book randomly at the pages mostly involving Francesca, and begins to read a few lines, then puts it on her belly, looks at me seriously and asks: *So, what will you do now?*
I breathe out a long sigh and answer: *I don't know, Valeria Maria, I don't know, I don't even know if I'll have time to do anything.*
She looks at me with tears in her eyes: *I'll not see you again.* By the

tone of her voice I know it's a statement and not a question. *Valeria Maria, you are the daughter I never had, but that life has given me; soon you'll get out of here and live the life you want, you'll decide for yourself, as it should be. I have lived my life and I have to thank life for every moment, for every joke and for letting me get this far. It's not true that you'll never see me again: if you really want, close your eyes and think... I'll be there.*

I go out and, without looking back, I head quickly to the Halls Foundation. There's nobody in the hall, I have some copies of my book with me; I walk slowly towards the huge circular corridor leading directly to the dome. From the monitors it's clear the show's already started up there; the New Year celebrations will last all night. On the third floor I notice an electric car moving slowly, I am astonished: Renzo's driving, at his side are Franco, and Gigi and Italo are on the back seat. I ask: *What are you doing here?* Renzo answers me: *Once a year we come here for a couple of days for our check-up, you know, at our age we need it.* I show them my book and ask: *Did they give you my book?*
Yes, says Renzo, showing me a still sealed book package, *but we'll look at it later, now we should go and look for something to eat.*
While he devours a gigantic croissant, the electric car disappears round a curve.

I keep on going up slowly, I don't know what's happening to me, I feel weak, my legs are trembling and my vision is blurred. From the screens I can see my photographs. I hear the speaker announcing *This evening we're also launching the book by Arturo Croci, who was our patient and who died five years ago while being treated by his French cardiologist. He wrote this book to pay tribute to the woman of his life...*

Everything turns black, my left leg won't support me anymore, I know I'm falling to the ground, but I don't feel anything underneath me, I just go down, down and I sink into total blackness.

Epilogue

I'm floating in blackness, it's soft, there's nothing, no joy, no pain, no emotion, no thought; I just know I exist, simply that.

I'm going upwards, the blackness is turning milky grey, there's an annoying white light all round me, I sense some movement near me, there's a luminous white shape that's moving. I'm unaware of time, slowly I focus on my surroundings, there's a dark-skinned boy, he's tanned, wearing a white jacket and trousers and latex gloves on his hands. Yes, he's the nurse I saw in the Barcelona hospital; he approaches and I murmur in Spanish: *Lo sé, te conozco, te vi en la clínica de cardiología de Barcelona.* (I recognise you; I saw you in the cardiology clinic in Barcelona.) He looks surprised and then exclaims: *Barcelona? Nonsense, we are in Bergamo!**

I close my eyes; I am confused; slowly, slowly, darkness absorbs me. From the depths I rise again to the surface, I open my eyes and... Francesca is next to my bed and holding my hand, I look at my arms, they are black, full of bruises; it really is Francesca's hand, she caresses my forehead and hair, and her touch, though far away, is so sweet. I close my eyes then and open them again; Francesca is really there, I'm totally astonished and my thoughts freeze, I can barely say: *Oh... but... weren't you dead?* Francesca looks at me surprised and exclaims: *Arturo, what are you saying?*

I ask: *Where... where... do you live now?* She looks at me worried: *Arturo, where d'you think I live? In my house!* Suddenly I realise that Francesca really is alive, it's all too much and I start crying; my tears are hot and blind me, they're not tears of pain, but of happiness. Francesca stays with me for a while and says: *You know, you're a warrior.*** *It's alright, now I have to go, but I'll come back to see you.*

Francesca turns to go away, and I start crying again, so she turns and says: *Come on, Arturo, if you carry on like that, you'll make everyone who loves you feel bad too.* I stop crying, I don't know what's happened to me exactly: it's like my leg, my left thigh, and also half my pelvis no longer exist; my nose is broken, I have bedsores on my head, my bottom and my feet, but I won't allow myself to become a burden to others and I swear that no one will ever see me crying again.

My friend Franco comes to see me, wearing a protective green gown, hat and mask. Later, I discovered that Franco had come to see me every day, while I was in coma. Franco talks to me half in the Bergamo dialect and half in Italian:
Ciao cum'e stet? (Hello, how are you?).
I reply: *I'm fine, Franco.* As a matter of fact, I don't really have any idea how I am; then he asks me:
Do you remember the meeting we had in the Riviera?
I reflect for a moment, then I say: *Are you talking about the first Florum in 1984 at the Grand Hotel del Mare in Bordighera?*
Franco smiles, turns to a window and shouts out slowly making each word count: *Hooray, his head is working!!!*
After a while Franco says: *You were talking about a book in the coma, even though you were intubated the nurses could understand what you were saying - 'I have to write the book' - I asked Aldo and he told me that you had to write a book for the University of Turin.*
I smile and close my eyes.

I sink back into the blackness, but this time it's different. I'm floating, there is no pain, and I'm aware that I can decide whether to let myself sink deeper into infinity or come back into the light. Francesca is alive, I want to choose life, I'll fight with all my strength to live, now that I know she's there: I WANT TO LIVE.

The battle to live and walk again was not easy at all. The week after my awakening was hell. The prolonged intubation had crushed my epiglottis, my throat burned continuously and they could not give me anything to drink. To everyone who approached my bed I was asking for *water, broth, whisky, coca cola, anything that's liquid!* After almost a month of coma my lungs were full of phlegm and I had a hard time expelling it. Nurses came from time to time to put a cannula into my lungs via my throat to suck it up; the pain was unbearable and I fainted every time. I would come to and say to myself: *I can do it, I can do it, she's alive!* After a week, a nurse gives me half a glass of water saying: *I know I can't quench your thirst, but drink slowly, in a while I'll give you some more.* My hands tremble as I bring the glass to my lips; I drink but my mouth and throat are numb.

Gina comes to see me with Valter and Luigi, she brings me my Christmas stocking; I try to open it to see what's in it, but my fingers are weak and don't respond to my commands. Wincing with pain but trying to smile, I ask her:
How much coal did you put in there? There were only chocolates. When Bruno enters I'm devastated, and say desperately:
Bruno, take me away from here, take me to Mocomero, he replies that he can't and I answer back: *Tomorrow is Saturday and they won't do anything over the weekend, you can bring me back here on Monday.*
He says: *Maybe you're right about that, but you have to stay here, don't worry, I'll come back to see you.*

After a month of coma and intensive care in Bergamo, I spent six months in a wheelchair at the Umberto I Hospital in Bellano; at that time the work on the magazine was mainly carried out by Aldo. Many people came to see me: Anna Jole, Angelo, Claudio, Charles, Franco, Gianni, Patricia, Valter, Vittorio... just to mention a few. Francesca often came to see me too and happily continues to live her life. My wife came to visit me every day during my seven months in hospital, she only stayed home on 26 February 2006: it had snowed so much that even the trains weren't running.

I have told Gina the story and she, from time to time, says:
I'm still waiting for my 60,000 euros.
When they let me out, I left hospital with two crutches, a brace and a support on my foot. I continued my physiotherapy for another four years at the Merate hospital. Even now I still continue physiotherapy with Stefania, a private physiotherapist who also treated me at the Bellano hospital.

I started writing Coma when I was hospitalised in Bellano, but after the episode in which Francesca was killed, I became blocked. I started again years later at Ban Kamala in Thailand. Many were surprised to see that the memory of my life in coma was so vivid. In Bellano, a nurse was so taken with the story that she asked her superiors to test me for HIV and hepatitis C which turned out to be negative.

Many people ask me if I saw luminous tunnels and I answer no, nothing of that kind: I simply slipped into blackness and I came back floating in blackness. When I think of that experience, all my certainties about reality are shaken.

The perception of time when we dream is dilated, in my case to such an extent that it allowed me to live a whole life. I tried to find a logical explanation that would allow me to consider everything rationally. The explanation is there and it's perfect, the effects of morphine, of the other drugs and the the mind always trying to find answers to any question. However, this answer does not totally convince me, as in that life my feelings, perceptions, joys, sorrows were absolutely real to me and equal to what I feel in this one.

I am therefore confused and uncertain, I don't know which life is true and which one a dream and maybe both are neither false nor true.

When I woke up some doctors said that I could never walk again, others that I was going to recover fully, others that my life was going to be very short.

The wisest and the most human was Maurizio Tespili, my cardiologist who told me:

When someone experiences something this serious, there can be three types of reaction: depression even worse than the illness itself; ignoring what has happened and thinking that everything will be the same as before; or being aware of what has happened and acting accordingly, so as to live your life well.

I have tried to do this last, to get the best from life and to give my best to the people I love.

My aorta split again in 2013, two days after my return from Udon Thani, where I'd been for the wedding of my friends Robert Zurel and Pia Parichat. Luckily for me, medicine had made great strides in eight years. They reconstructed my aorta and I was intubated. Five operations in 45 days and this time the people I have to thank are so many, from Giordano Tasca to Michele Triggiani, from

Aldo Stefano Ferrari, who every now and then gives me advice, to all my cardiologists, Pierfranco Ravizza and the entire nursing team of Lecco Hospital.

In this book there are some episodes I actually lived in this life and which I simply recalled in the other. Others, on the other hand, have been lived exclusively in the other dimension. Over the years, some of those facts have since come true. Today I happily spend my life between Calco, Mocomero-Castelletto, Marsala, Buenos Aires and Ban Kamala. At the end of this book I would like to thank all the people and they really are very numerous who have been close to me and have *breathed life into my life*.
Viva la vita

Ban Kamala, 19 March 2018.

Notes
* *I was in a coma from 15 December 2005 to 4 January 2006. On 4 January, my 'awakening' began: it was gradual and I fully awake by 9 January. My medical records for 4 January note: 'vigilant, in a confused state.'*

** *Francesca refers to the 'warrior' mentioned by Juan Matus in the books by Carlos Castaneda. 'A man approaches knowledge as if he were going to war: perfectly vigilant, with fear, respect and absolute security.' 'The difference between a warrior and a common man is that the common man takes everything as either a blessing or a disaster, while the warrior takes everything as a challenge and challenges are neither good nor bad: they are simply challenges...'*

About the author

Arturo Croci is a journalist and writer with a diploma in horticulture from Minoprio, Como.
He studied philosophy at the University of Barcelona.
Coma, which includes sections of his previous publications, is his first full-length work.

Publications

1994 - I giardini di Lhasa (*The gardens of Lhasa*), in *Il ritorno di Re Arcobaleno*, AAVV, artisti di Orizzonti Aperti, Ace International.
1995 - *A Mar Parà*, and *Sulle orme di Livingstone* (In the footsteps of Livingstone), in *Il volo di Icaro*, artists of Orizzonti Aperti, Ace International.
1995 - Poems, in *Ali*, Danilo Manenti and Monica Malzani, Ace International.
1999 - *Instant Creations*, poems of the musical CD of Andrea Ortu and Pier Paderni, ed. Time Bandits.
2016 - *Navigare*, AAVV, poems, Pagine, Roma
2019 - Poems, in *Ritorni*, Monica Malzani, Silvia Leggio, Pier Paderni, Make Art not War.

Acknowledgements

Thanks to: Patricia Borlenghi, Aldo Colombo, Anna Bianca Galvani, Celestina Galvani, Claudio Carrai, John Eric Jackson and Remo Varani.

Printed in September 2019
by Rotomail Italia S.p.A., Vignate (MI) - Italy